Complex Criminality

AF781534

Complex Criminality

D. Abels, D. Bruin & H. van der Wilt (eds.)

eleven
international publishing

Published, sold and distributed by Eleven International Publishing

P.O. Box 85576
2508 CG The Hague
The Netherlands
Tel.: +31 70 33 070 33
Fax: +31 70 33 070 30
e-mail: sales@elevenpub.nl
www.elevenpub.com

Sold and distributed in USA and Canada
International Specialized Book Services
920 NE 58th Avenue, Suite 300
Portland, OR 97213-3786, USA
Tel: 1-800-944-6190 (toll-free)
Fax: +1-503-280-8832
orders@isbs.com
www.isbs.com

Eleven International Publishing is an imprint of Boom uitgevers Den Haag.

ISBN 978-94-6236-713-5
ISBN 978-94-6274-622-0 (E-book)

© 2016 D. Abels, D. Bruin & H. van der Wilt (eds.) | Eleven International Publishing

This publication is protected by international copyright law.
All rights reserved. No part of this publication may be reproduced, stored in a retrieval system, or transmitted in any form or by any means, electronic, mechanical, photocopying, recording or otherwise, without the prior permission of the publisher.

Printed in The Netherlands

Table of contents

Complex Criminality – an introduction

Denis Abels[1]

This book presents a collection of essays on complex criminality. These essays were written for a national gathering of PhD candidates at the University of Amsterdam on 6 June 2014. Complex criminality, which was the theme of that gathering and is the title of this book, calls for a definition. Is not, after all, all criminality complex? Do not all legal dealings with criminality involve a complex factual and normative analysis of occurrences? And does conduct that is labelled as criminal not practically always involve a complex mixture of, partly interacting non-personal and personal circumstances?

So how can criminality not be considered complex?

Neither does it help to focus on the meaning of the term 'complex' if one wishes to get a clearer view of this book's subject. Aside from 'complicated', or perhaps 'multi-layered', or 'multi-dimensional', the adjective 'complex' may have the meaning of 'sophisticated', which may at first blush appear difficult to apply to criminality, at least perhaps until one thinks of financial or economic criminality.

'Complex' may further refer to some activity that entangles, or complicates subject matter that to an outsider or a lay person does not necessarily seem complex. We often encounter such activity in criminal law. Just like practitioners of other disciplines, criminal lawyers translate a certain factual complex into their own jargon and thereby reduce or interpret facts in such a manner that those directly involved in the factual occurrences may feel alienated from the outcome of such an interpretation or translation.

'Complex' may yet have another meaning, *i.e.*, when used, as a substantive, in the phrase 'the military-industrial complex'. If understood in this sense, complex does not refer to the complicated, or sophisticated nature of the criminality, nor to the activities of lawyers translating seemingly non-complicated subject-matter into legal jargon. It rather refers to the systemic nature of its object.

---

[1] Mr. Dr. D. Abels is associate professor at the Criminal law department of the University of Amsterdam.

Systemic, then, in connection to criminality, may be understood in at least three different ways. First, it may refer to the context in which criminal acts are committed, a context which may be characteristic or even a constitutive element of specific crimes; a context that may consist of, for instance, a State or a multi-layered organization, one which has certain purposes and officials working for it, occupying different roles or functions. This is what in international criminal law is meant by 'system criminality', *i.e.*, the 'phenomenon that international crimes – notably crimes against humanity, genocide and war crimes – are often caused by collective entities in which the individual authors of these acts are embedded'.[2]

Second, systemic may assume the ordinary meaning of 'system' as listed in the Oxford Dictionary, *i.e.* 'a set of things working together as parts of a mechanism or an interconnecting network; a complex whole'. An example would be the digestive system. The emphasis is hereby placed on the operational aspect: the functioning of the whole depends on the cooperation of the parts. If we shift our focus from criminality to criminal justice, then this interpretation of the term systemic makes sense as well. We simply need to look at the contributions of the various stages and agents of the criminal justice process to the system's eventual output. Such an output has qualitative and quantitative aspects like, for example, a completed trial that may be labelled just, or the punishment of persons found guilty of committing an offence.[3] But there appears to be something more to criminal justice than mere output defined in qualitative and quantitative terms. After all, output defined as 'punishment of those found guilty', even if that presumes the existence of reliable fact-finding and a fair criminal procedure, still remains rather vague. It does not say anything about the objectives of such punishment, or about what binds the justice apparatus together, aside from a shared strive for a certain output defined in terms of quality and efficiency.

A third meaning of the term 'systemic' may provide some further guidance. Complex may assume the meaning, also listed in the Oxford Dictionary, of 'a set of principles or procedures according to which something is done; an organized scheme or method'. It is not difficult at all to see how the phrase '*procedures* according to which something is done' is relevant to criminal justice and, more specifically, to the law of criminal procedure. Examples are evidence law and regulations governing unlawfully obtained evidence.

---

[2] A. Nollkaemper, 'Introduction', in: A. Nollkaemper and H. van der Wilt, *System Criminality in International Law*, Cambridge: Cambridge University Press 2009, p. 1-25, at 1.

[3] These qualitative and quantitative aspects can, of course, not be completely separated in a criminal justice apparatus governed by the rule of law in a democratic society.

It would be more challenging to apply the phrase 'a set of *principles* according to which something is done' to criminal justice. Is there a set of principles that bind together criminal justice, all of its agents, and all of its stages? When searching for such principles, it might be convenient to link up with notions are usually referred to for this very reason, *i.e.*, the notions of retribution and prevention as overarching goals of criminal justice. If, however, retribution were the main principle, or objective, guiding the legislature when establishing sanctioning norms, would this necessarily require its expression an application in the other, subsequent stages of criminal justice? Back in 1975, Jonkers argued that, for a proper understanding of penal principles, a distinction must be made between the levels of legislation, application (by which he meant sentencing) and execution.[4] According to him, these levels are not strictly separated. The level of execution refers to that of application which, in turn, refers to that of the legislature. The lower level should always take into account the aims governing the higher level(s).[5] More contemporary scholars have, however, argued that the execution stage does neither look back at the sentencing phase, nor at the legislature's purposes of punishment, but is rather forward looking, thereby assuming a character that differs from criminal justice's other phases or stages. They recognize the existence of a relative autonomy that exists between the principles and purposes that guide sentencing judges and those that govern the enforcement stage.[6]

It may, therefore, be doubted that there exists some bunch of principles that can or ought to guide the whole gamut of criminal justice, which would render criminal justice a system under the third meaning of 'systemic'.[7] In other words: although *complex* criminal justice, may be understood as a *system* according the first and second meaning of systemic as described above, this does not yet imply that 'one size fits all' principles can be applied to all the different aspects and stages of criminal justice.

What transpires from the foregoing thoughts, is that 'complex criminality' is a very broad notion with many distinct meanings, *e.g.*, complicated criminality, which may actually apply to all forms of criminality, sophisticated criminality, common facts

---

[4] W.H.A. Jonkers, 'De strafrechtelijke straf: inhoud, grondslag, doeleinden', in: Y. Buruma (ed.), *100 Jaar Strafrecht. Klassieke teksten van de twintigste eeuw*, Amsterdam: Amsterdam University Press 1999, p. 163-176.

[5] W.H.A. Jonkers, 'De strafrechtelijke straf: inhoud, grondslag, doeleinden', in: Y. Buruma (ed.), *100 Jaar Strafrecht. Klassieke teksten van de twintigste eeuw*, Amsterdam: Amsterdam University Press 1999, p. 163-176, at 174.

[6] D. van Zyl Smit & S. Snacken, *Principles of European Prison Law and Policy*, Oxford: Oxford University Press 2009, p. 76.

[7] See, more detail, Denis Abels, 'Limiting the Objectives of the Enforcement of International Punishment', in: Róisín Mulgrew and Denis Abels (eds.), *Research Handbook on the International Penal System*, Edward Elgar Publishing 2016.

rendered more difficult to understand for lay persons as a result of a translation into criminal legal jargon, or the systemic nature of certain crimes. This wide diversity of understandings is exemplified by the papers contained in this book, which cover a wide range of topics while they, nonetheless, all deal with complex criminality.

The Dutch law on drugs

Deborah Bruin[1]

Introduction

In 1998 the UN formulated the following as one of its goals: '*...to devote particular attention to the measures for the control of precursors, adopted at the present session, and further decide to establish the year 2008 as a target date for States, with a view to eliminating or reducing significantly the illicit manufacture, marketing and trafficking of psychotropic substances, including synthetic drugs, and the diversion of precursors.*'[2]

The Political Declaration, of which the foregoing citation was taken, assumed that it is possible to eliminate or reduce significantly the manufacturing, marketing and trafficking of drugs within 10 years. This would make it possible to arrive at a 'drugs-free world' in 2008.[3] It is needless to say that the drugs-free world was not reached in 2008. In 2009, after the evaluation of the Political Declaration of 1998, a new 10 year drug-strategy was formulated. 2019 was mentioned as the new date for the elimination or significant reduction of cultivation, manufacturing, marketing, and trafficking of drugs.[4]

The international conventions of the UN have played a leading role in determining the international and national policies regarding drugs. Since the birth of the so

---

[1] Deborah Bruin, PhD candidate University of Amsterdam.

[2] General Assembly, S-20/2. Political Declaration, twentieth special session 10 June 1998, A/RES/S-20/2, 21 October 1998.

[3] Although the 'drug-free world' is not mentioned in the Political Declaration, it was the underlying theme of the twentieth session and it was mentioned by the Under-Secretary-General Pino Arlacchi: '*Let us all go forward with the resolve that the commitment we have made to work for a drug-free world will be met with actions and the resources needed to ensure real and measurable results. Together we can meet this challenge. Now, let's get to work.*' Ninth plenary meeting during the twentieth special session of the United Nations General Assembly, 10 June 1998, New York, A/S-20/PV.9, p. 25.

[4] UNODC, *Political Declaration and Plan of Action on International Cooperation towards an Integrated and Balanced Strategy to Counter the World Drug Problem*, High-level segment of the fifty-second session of the Commission on Narcotic Drugs, held on the 11th and 12th of March 2009 in Vienna.

called Dutch model,[5] there has been an ongoing debate about the possibilities to develop national policies, and limitation of the possibility to develop national and local policies by international conventions. This ongoing debate[6] on international limits on domestic policies through conventions and other regulations by the EU and UN, complicates a subject that is already difficult to reach any political agreement on, i.e., drugs.[7]

This paper focuses on the complexity of the policy of drugs, with the Dutch model as an example. Because of the limited amount of pages I have for this contribution, there is no room to discuss all possible complicating factors like, for example, the absence of victims who report drugs offences to the police, the involvement of criminal organizations and drug related cross-border criminality. These factors can be complicating to the making of law and enforcement of law on drugs. This paper will describe the Dutch model and specifically three of the aspects of the Dutch model that render drugs related criminality a complex area of criminal law par excellence, the policymaking on different levels, the cooperation between different areas of law, and the partial regulation of cannabis within the Dutch model.

The first aspect of drugs related criminality that renders this type of criminality complex is that the policymaking takes place on three levels: international, domestic and local. The second factor is the cooperation, or lack thereof, between two different areas of law, i.e., administrative and criminal law; areas with their own rules and principles, which have a distinct impact on creating and enforcing the law on drugs.[8] The third factor concerns the fact that the Dutch model' is the result of a political compromise.[9] In this model, the sale of cannabis is not prosecuted if the applicable rules are followed, but the growing of cannabis as production for the sale is prohibited.

---

[5] The Dutch model is described in par. 1.2.1. This term covers the Dutch policy in which cannabis is forbidden (by law), but offences related to cannabis are not prosecuted under certain circumstances (based on directives).

[6] Van Kempen & Fedorova 2014.

[7] In footnote 45 you can find an example of the division within the political parties of our current government when it concerns voting on the subject of drugs.

[8] The cooperation or lack of cooperation between administrative and criminal within the law on drugs is the main subject of the PhD thesis I am currently working on at the University of Amsterdam.

[9] More about this in par. 1.2.1.

1. Three level policy making

1.1 The beginnings of an international drugs policy

In 1909, the first Opium conference was held in Singapore.[10] This occasion marks the beginning of an international policy on drugs. Before this conference, there had already been some discussion on the risks of drugs being freely available and being provided for by unschooled pharmacists. Some countries introduced laws to warn people for the dangers of the use of drugs. Some substances had to be labelled as poisons and pharmacists were obliged to be educated on drugs.[11] The conference in Singapore turned out to be the early beginnings of an international cooperation on drugs policy. Initially the focus was on Opium, but soon it shifted to other drugs.[12]

After the Singapore conference, several conventions were adopted constituting international drugs policy. The first was the International Opium Convention of January 1912. On the 11th and 19th of February 1925, the Conventions of Geneva were established, followed by the conventions of 1931 and the 1936. The next convention is still very relevant to international drug policy and in fact replaced all previous conventions. This convention is the Single Convention of New York of 1961 (hereafter: SC). After the SC, two more followed. These are the conventions of 1971 and 1988 and they were meant to supplement the SC.

These conventions limit the scope and prescribe to a certain extent the content of domestic national drug policy. The beginnings of the Dutch national drug policy were not grounded in some domestic initiative, but constituted implementations of the international conventions.[13]

1.2 From international to domestic drug policy

The Dutch law on drugs is still called the 'Opiumwet' (Opium legislation), although it now covers more than just opium. This name was given to the first Dutch

[10] The Shanghai Opium Commission met from the 5th to the 26th of February on initiative of the USA. Buxton 2008, p. 7; Musto 1987, p. 35-37.
[11] Musto 1987, chapter 4; Buxton 2008.
[12] Cannabis was added in the *International Opium Convention*, 19 February 1925.
[13] The limitations are described in par. 1.4.For a more detailed description of the conventions I refer to the extensive literature. For example: Bewley-Taylor 2012.

domestic legislation on drugs in 1919,[14] which was a direct consequence of the convention on Opium from 1912. In the early beginnings of the international drug policy, the main focus was on Opium.[15] The Dutch drugs legislation of 1928 was a direct consequence of the conventions of 1925. Although much has changed since 1928, that domestic legislation still constitutes the basis of the Dutch domestic drug policy.[16]

1.2.1 Domestic policy: the Dutch model

The Dutch policy on drugs differentiates between possession for use and possession for trade, and considers the latter as more deserving of punishment. Second the Dutch policy on drugs differentiates between the various substances, because of the different risks they carry.[17] Hard drugs are the drugs that present a higher risk of damage to health and society; soft drugs carry a lower risk and are therefore deserving of a different approach. There are several arguments that can be made for these differentiations, but the main one is grounded in the 'risk-thought' and the related call for separation of the hard- and soft drugs markets. The 'risk-thought' is the idea that substances carrying different risks to health and society should be treated differently. In this way, it is possible to create a controlled environment for those who are 18 years or older for them to be able to experiment with a drug that is not as damaging as hard drugs. This controlled environment entails the availability

[14] This was the first repressive law on drugs which intended to prohibit certain drug related acts. Before we had a law on Absinth, a law concerning the free distribution of drugs by unschooled pharmacists, and of course the Opium related rules that were meant to give the Dutch government a monopoly on the production and selling of Opium.

[15] Several reasons can be given to explain this focus on Opium. The trading position of China where the use of opium was more common is one reason. Another reason can be found in the history of the instigator of the development of the international drug policy: the USA. After winning the war against Spain the USA gained the Philippines, Cuba, Guam and Puerto Rico in 1898, determined in the convention of Paris. The USA now had to make a decision about the many opium selling points that the Spanish established on the Philippines. The idea that they couldn't fight the opium problem alone but needed the help of the international community was born: Musto 1987, p. 25-28.

[16] For example the punishments changed, substances were added, but also new articles are added. For example article 13b, given the mayor the authority to close any premises, house, or yard, where drugs listed in the Opium law are sold, given over or provided, or are present for these purposes.

[17] These differentiations are also known as: the double two-track policy. The risk of hard-drugs justifies a harder punishment, the possession for trade and trade and growth are punished harder as well, therefore the trade of Hard-drugs is punished harder than the possession for use of hard-drugs. This double two track policy was introduced in 1976. More about this (in Dutch): Blom 1998; Blom 2015.

of qualified personnel and information and does not allow for contact with hard drugs. This differentiation between risks of hard and soft drugs use, and between the possession for use or for trade, finds expression in Dutch law through separate penalty clauses and differentiation in punishment. The introduction of these differentiations by legislation was the result of a political compromise, since there existed no political majority that supported a complete regulation or legalization of cannabis. The compromise was found in the fact that the trade in drugs and hard drugs related offences would be threatened with more severe sentences, while a more lenient approach were to be taken towards the possession of drugs for own use and towards soft drugs related offences.[18]

The Dutch model refers to the model that is applied in the Netherlands in which the selling of cannabis in a so-called 'coffeeshop' is prohibited but in which such acts are not prosecuted if the relevant legal conditions are being honored. These conditions are the so-called AHOJGI+ criteria: no advertising, no hard-drugs, no nuisance, no minors, no more than 5 grams a day per person, and selling is restricted to residents of Dutch municipals.[19]

The final condition was introduced as a pilot in the city of Maastricht in 2005.[20] It was intended to make coffeeshops less appealing to foreign tourists who come to the Netherlands to buy and/or use drugs. These so-called drug tourists may contribute to traffic and parking problems, and may create noise pollution. Since 2013, the I-condition is part of national policy,[21] although drug tourism is not an issue in most

[18] In Dutch: Blom 1998, p. 85; De Kort 1995, p. 245-246.
[19] These conditions can be found in the directive Opiumlaw: Aanwijzing Opiumwet, *Staatscourant* 2015, 5391.
[20] Decision of the municipal council on the 20th December 2005, article 2.3.1.1 and following of the 'General Local Regulation' Maastricht 2006. This Pilot named after Donner, the minister of Justice at that time, contained the rule that only Dutch people were allowed to enter a coffeeshop. The rule was declared void by the court of appeal because local authorities cannot make rules about the same subjects, and with the same purposes as the national government. Higher national law outranks lower local law. Afdeling bestuursrechtspraak Raad van State 29th of June 2011, *Jurisprudentie Bestuursrecht* 2011/250 with annotation R.J.B. Schutgens.
[21] The I condition stands for '*ingezetene*', which is the Dutch word for resident. Since the 1st of January 2013 it is part of the directive Opium law: Aanwijzing Opiumwet, *Staatscourant* 2015, 5391. Unlike the pilot Donner it doesn't prohibit non Dutch people from entering coffeeshops, but requires visitors of a coffeeshop to be a resident of a Dutch municipal. Allowing only Dutch people would be a direct violation of the first article of our constitution which contains the equality principle and the prohibition to discriminate. So they changed it to residents of a Dutch municipal, which is considered to be a bit less discriminating than allowing only Dutch people. This (changed) rule was introduced on the 1st of May 2012 in the southern regions: Noord-Brabant, Zeeland and Limburg.

municipals in the Netherlands. In most municipals the I -condition is introduced in local policy, but is not being enforced.[22]

The I-condition was introduced together with the condition that the coffeeshop must be a closed club that can only serve customers who are registered as members. A coffeeshop is not permitted to have more than 2000 members. This condition was intended to make coffeeshops smaller and more controllable. This 'closed club condition' was abandoned shortly after its introduction in the southern part of the Netherlands.[23] People refused to register and turned to illegal dealers or coffeeshops located more to the North where registration was not required because the rule was not being enforced.

The plus in AHOJGI+ makes clear that these conditions can be supplemented by any other conditions that the local authorities may wish to apply. Conditions like 'no alcohol' or 'no coffeeshops in the vicinity of secondary and special primary schools' are being applied in some municipals.

1.3 Role of the local authorities

When the Dutch model as described above came into being,[24] its rules were established by the national central authorities: the legislature decided on the differentiation between possession for use and for trade, and also on the differentiation between hard and soft drugs. The policy choice to not prosecute for the selling and possession for the own use of soft drugs in coffeeshops under certain conditions is laid down by the central public prosecution agency in its directives.[25] The main goal of this national policy when it was introduced was to protect and stimulate public health. To serve this purpose, a so called 'housedealer' was allowed to trade in youth centers and was not prosecuted for selling cannabis unless a decision was made by the mayor, head of police and head of the prosecution of the local area to the contrary.[26] These three authorities combined are known as the 'local triangle'. The local triangle has no explicit powers to make decisions, but is meant

---

[22] A famous example is Amsterdam. This town does deal with a lot of nuisance by (drug)tourists. The mayor and council prefer to deal with the nuisances by taking other precautions, but they do not choose to implement the I-criteria.
[23] On the 1st of January 2013 it was removed from the directive.
[24] Introduced by the change in the Opiumlaw in 1976, and the directives of 1976 and 1978. Blom 1998; Blom 2015.
[25] The 'College van Procureurs-Generaal' can make general directives or give directions in a specific case to the prosecution, based on article 130 section 4 of the 'Law on Judicial Organisation' (Wet op de Rechterlijke Organisatie).
[26] Blom 1998, p. 89-90; De Kort 1995, p. 254-256.

as an advising organ within which the coordination between these three participants is made possible.

In the 90s, the housedealer had developed into the phenomenon of the coffeeshop, i.e. into more organized selling points. The focus of public policy thereby shifted from public health to a fight against nuisances and disturbances in the vicinity of coffeeshops. Like sound pollution or nuisances experiences by illegal parking. Local authorities became more involved in the policy on drugs and established their own local policies, in which they decided on how many coffeeshops they allowed, if at all, and on the applicable rules and conditions.[27]

1.4 Hierarchy, limitations and complications

The description above shows the three levels involved in the determination and enforcement of the policy on drugs: International, domestic and local. On international level, the SC of 1961 is a highly important convention, which obliges states to criminalize certain acts concerning drugs not including acts with a medical or scientific goal or purpose.[28]

At the highest level, we find the international drug policy. Conventions predominate Dutch domestic law according to the Articles 93 and 94 of the Dutch Constitution. The question whether the Dutch model is in alliance with the conventions, is the object of much scholarly debate and has been answered differently by different authors.

Related to such debates is the question whether the Dutch model may be complemented by no longer prosecuting for the growing, transport and buying of cannabis by a coffeeshop in order to resolve the dichotomy that is inherent to the current model. Under the current Dutch model, solely the sale by coffeeshops to customers is not being prosecuted. The growing, transportation, keeping of stash and buying of cannabis by the coffeeshop does not form part of the model and is being prosecuted for. When the Dutch model was introduced in 1976-1978, it was intended to be a temporary solution until the moment that there would be a political majority to decide on whether or not to regulate the whole of the cannabis chain, i.e., from production to sale. Forty years later, the Dutch still suffer from the fact that the

[27] This shift from national policy to a national and local policy is subject of my final thesis: Bruin 2011.

[28] Single Convention of Narcotic drugs, New York 1961, as changed by the protocol of 1972. Article 4 gives the general aims of the convention and article 36 gives the obligation to criminalize certain acts.

model finds its basis in a political compromise as a result of which only the selling of cannabis by coffeeshops is being regulated, which leaves the Dutch with an inherently contradictory, or 'half' policy.[29]

The main argument for not regulating the matter further lies in the limitations provided by international policy.

1.4.1 International versus domestic

As mentioned above, the SC provides for some of the most important limits on the freedom of States to organize their own drug policy. It prescribes states to limit any permissible actions regarding drugs to actions with a medical or scientific purpose. Actions that don't serve these purposes are to be criminalized according to article 36. Article 36 section 4 states that: '*Nothing contained in this article shall affect the principle that the offences to which it refers shall be defined, prosecuted and punished in conformity with the domestic law of a Party.*'

Under Dutch law, however, the prosecution generally has the freedom and authority to decide on whether or not to prosecute. When it comes to the selling of cannabis by coffeeshops under certain conditions, such acts are not prosecuted based on a general directive.[30] Under Dutch law, prosecution is the prerogative of the prosecutor, and is not something he is obliged to do.[31]

I am of the opinion that such directives are permitted under the SC.[32] First, the wording of article 36 section 4 SC allows for such regulations. The Dutch comply

---

[29] Recently the question if there are any possibilities under the international conventions to regulate the buying, transportation, stashing or growing of cannabis and thus complete the Dutch model, has been researched again: Van Kempen & Fedorova 2014; Van Kempen & Fedorova 2016.

[30] The 'College van Procureurs-Generaal' can make general directives or give directions in a specific case to the prosecution, based on article 130 section 4 of the 'Law on Judicial Organisation' (Wet op de Rechterlijke Organisatie). Based on that article there is a general directive Opiumlaw, as mentioned before: Aanwijzing Opiumwet, *Staatscourant* 2015, 5391. The freedom of the prosecution to choose to prosecute or not is based on articles 167 and 242 section 2 of the Dutch Code on Criminal Procedure.

[31] Article 161 section 2 and article 242 section 2 of the Dutch Criminal Procedural code.

[32] See a different conclusion in: Van Kempen & Fedorova 2014. I do totally agree with them that the regulation of cannabis for recreational use is not something that the creators of the SC wanted to be possible. And although using the intention of the makers is a very valid and necessary method to interpret the text of the convention, I disagree with the conclusion that because of the intention it is not possible to regulate anything else than we currently do. If the text of the SC provides space to regulate the sell like we do now in the Dutch model, than

with the demand of criminalization, although certain acts are not being prosecuted in accordance with domestic law. If regulating the selling is permitted under the SC, than the same applies to the growing and transportation.[33]

A common misunderstanding is that the use of cannabis is legal in the Netherlands. It is not. The Dutch fulfilled their obligation under the SC to criminalize the use and selling of cannabis under domestic law. The Dutch merely chose to not prosecute certain acts committed under certain circumstances, which is in accordance with Paragraph 4 of Article 36 SC, which allows member States to prosecute and punish according to domestic law.

The Dutch model only covers the recreational use of cannabis. The medical and industrial use of cannabis are allowed under the SC. Accordingly, cannabis that is distributed by pharmacies as a 'medical cannabis' is completely legal under the Dutch law on drugs.[34] The Dutch law on drugs prohibits all acts regarding cannabis, even industrial cannabis or hemp that is not fit for recreational or medicinal use. An exemption for the growing of industrial hemp is made in the 'Opiumwetbesluit'.[35]

1.4.2 International limitations to domestic policy: the example of Bolivia

The limitations to the freedom of States to determine domestic policy are not necessarily problematic. But they can become so where, for example, new insights call for new measures for which the old and static conventions leave no scope, i.e., no scope for renewal or for the adaptation to domestic needs. Those needs may differ between states, which calls for the possibility of distinct approaches.

---

other regulations are possible as well. It is one way or the other. Also limiting the space the text gives, based on the comments of the makers, reflecting the out dated view on cannabis from 1960, doesn't serve the reality of the problems we face in enforcing a paradoxal policy. But this was not part of the research assignment, so logically the authors didn't take this into account. They recently researched the subject again, adding different aspects to the research question, thereby adding to their previous research: Van Kempen & Fedorova 2016.

[33] There are extra rules when it comes to the growing of cannabis (art. 23 and 28 of the SC). The SC obliges the government to have a monopoly on growing cannabis, for the sake of total control. We can comply with that and still regulate. We already grow 'state weed' for medical purposes. The Opiumlaw actually orders the minister to grow enough cannabis for the medical supply of cannabis and scientific experiments, art. 8h of the Opiumlaw.

[34] Cannabis has three functions: Industrial, medicinal and recreational. Although they all belong to the same family the use and therefore the policy differs. Industrial cannabis is used for making canvas, paper, plastic, oil, food and many more. Industrial cannabis is usually called hemp, even though hemp is an old word for cannabis. It has 0,3 % or less THC, which is one of the main psychoactive component. This is the main difference with the cannabis for recreational and medicinal use, in which the THC percentage is higher.

[35] Last changes were made in January 2013. Last official publication can be found in: *Staatsblad*, 2012, 550.

An example is Bolivia, where coca leaves are not only grown for illegal trade, but also for their cultural use: for chewing, or making tea. Growing coca is legal in certain areas of Bolivia under certain conditions. This is allowed under the SC, which contains an exemption under Article 49 concerning specifically the chewing of coca leaves, but only under strict conditions. The provision was meant to be a temporarily one, a 25 year transition period was granted in article 49 paragraph 2 section.

The chewing of coca leaves is in no way to be compared to the snorting of cocaine. The former's effect and damage are minimal. It concerns a cultural habit in certain regions in South Amerika. The SC did not, however, allow for the legalization of the growing of coca plants specifically aimed at providing for the supply for this cultural habit. After the country's failed attempts to amend article 49, Bolivia denounced the SC[36]only to later on again accede to the convention, but this time with a reservation as regards the chewing of coca leaves and growing of coca leaves for that purpose.[37]

1.4.3 International limitations to domestic policy: the Dutch model

The more states that are involved in drafting a convention, the more difficult its establishment and the finding of common ground become. Once a convention is established, it is therefore understandable that states tend to hang on to it, even where new developments or research ask for its alteration. The Dutch law on drugs is supposed to serve the public health. Currently, however, it is not possible to control the quality of the cannabis available in coffeeshops and thereby protect the health of users, since only the selling of cannabis is regulated by law. The growing, transportation and other acts necessary for a coffeeshop owner to sell cannabis are prohibited, prosecuted and not regulated in anyway.[38]

The SC is often used as an excuse for not regulating anything else than the selling by coffeeshops. There are, for example, no checks as regards or limitation on the use of

---

[36] TNI, fact sheet: Coca leaves and the UN control, 2012. In march 2009 the government proposed a amendment of the SC. When that didn't work out they denounced the SC.

[37] <https://www.unodc.org/unodc/en/frontpage/2013/January/bolivia-to-re-accede-to-un-drug-convention-while-making-exception-on-coca-leaf-chewing.html>

[38] There is a legislative proposal that suggest changing the Dutch law on drugs, in order to regulate coffeeshops not only in a directive, but also in the law itself. This proposal suggests to regulate the whole chain of cannabis, from seed to sell. *Kamerstukken II*, 2014-2015, 34 165, nr. 2.

pesticides or substances that make the cannabis heavier.[39] If public health issues are not dealt with because of a convention that was meant to ban the negative effects of drugs use and addiction, then such a convention stands in the way of the achievement of its own purposes.[40] If a convention is based on the idea that severe punishment and repression are the best weapons in the war on drugs, and these turn out to be not that effective after all, then one should be able to alter its provisions, or at least rethink their interpretation.

From the 19th till the 21st of April 2016, a UNGASS meeting on drugs is planned in New York city.[41] If there is a right time and place to rethink the convention, this is it.

1.4.4 Complicating factors

The earlier mentioned stratified policy making does make creating a cohesive policy and enforcing the policy more complicated. Not just because policy on lower levels finds its limits in higher levels' policy. But also because in order to get a clear view of the entire drugs policy, one needs to have knowledge of all three levels. Each level has its own rules and system. This may lead to different approaches on the different levels. The rules on hierarchy between the different levels prevent disorder were the distinct levels to try to regulate the same matter. Complications which remain concern those caused by the more essential differences between the levels such as, for example, differences in goals, means, principles, enforcement possibilities, strategies, and differences regarding procedures which lead to distinct ease by which a system may adapt to new developments. This may lead to internal

---

[39] Since cannabis is sold based on quality and weight some cannabis is made heavier with e.g. soda's like sprite. The sugar will make the cannabis heavier and look whiter, which can be misinterpreted as a sign of strength since it looks like THC which also gives a white glow/layer on the cannabis.

[40] To illustrate this I want to point out the following document and citation: UNODC, Drug policy provisions from the international drug control Conventions, E/CN.7/2014/CRP.5, p. 1: '*Although the Conventions restrict the use of controlled drugs to medical and scientific purposes, this limitation should not be considered as the justification for a repressive "prohibitionist" regime, but as the foundation of a drug control system protecting the health of people from the inappropriate use of narcotic drugs and psychotropic substances.*' <http:/www.unodc.org/documents/commissions/CND/CND_Sessions/CND_57/E-CN7-2014-CRP05_V1400819_E.pdf>

[41] The meeting has its own website: <http://idpc.net/policy-advocacy/the-un-general-assembly-special-session-on-drugs-ungass-2016>. UNGASS stands for: United Nations General Assembly Special Session. This special session on drugs was originally planned for 2019, the year the 10 year drugs strategy ends and is evaluated. Multiple states have requested to have this meeting sooner.

conflicts or gaps within the whole of the drug policy. If different goals apply to the different levels, than that may complicate the synchronization of the policy as a whole, leaving room for inefficiency and paradoxes within the total policy. As said, because of the hierarchy between the different levels of rulemaking, the lower level must abide by the boundaries set by the higher level. This applies to the relationship between the international and the domestic level, but also between the national and local level. The latter will be discussed in the next paragraph.

1.5 National and local

Complications caused by the circumstance that the policy on drugs is developed and enforced on three different levels may occur not only as regards the relationship between the international and domestic, but also as regards that between the national and local level. Based on the Dutch constitution and law international predominates over domestic policy whilst national policy predominates local policy. As was stated in the previous paragraph, the rules on hierarchy do not solve all problems. In this paragraph, I discuss two complications that have arisen in the Netherlands and that concern the relationship between the national and local level. The first concerns the flexibility of the national policy and the room it leaves for adaptation of local policy to specific circumstances. The second concerns the phenomenon that different areas of law regulate both national and local policy.

1.5.1 The central government and local authorities

Dutch national policy consists of the law on drugs and directives for the prosecution that leave room to the coffeeshops for the selling of cannabis, and to individuals for the possession of cannabis under certain conditions.[42]

As the Dutch model developed from 1976 onwards, the local authorities started playing a bigger role in the determination and enforcement of the policy on drugs. In the nineties the policy's focus on drugs shifted from protecting the public health to

---

[42] The possession for own use of cannabis is limited to 5 grams or 5 plants. The possession of other drugs for own use is not prosecuted as well. The directive Opium law states that aiding or offering rehabilitation to the user is more important than prosecution. In addition the quantities of several drugs that are considered to be possession for own use are stated in the aforementioned directive Opium law and also the guidelines for prosecution of hard drugs: *Staatscourant* 2015, 4953.

the fight against (drug related) nuisance. The shifting of this focus can be explained by an exponential growth of the number of coffeeshops. Because of the increase in coffeeshops, it became evident that the nuisance caused by coffeeshops should be subject to stricter regulation. Local authorities wanted more discretion to decide whether they would have coffeeshops in their municipality or not, and, if so, how many.

Local authorities have what we call 'local autonomy'. This means that they are free in making rules and policy concerning their municipality, as long as these rules and policies belong to the municipal realm and are not covered by higher law or do not contradict higher law.[43] They are also entitled to make additional rules (on top of the national policy) to adapt the policy on drugs to local circumstances. The municipality of Amsterdam, for example, faces another situation than a small village in the middle of the Netherlands which has no lure for tourists.

The local policy must stay within the limits of national policy.[44] The main complication is the tension between making a national and general policy, which is clear, accessible and applies equally to all people and places, and the possibility to take measures locally to assure certain local needs are met. For example the above mentioned I-condition, that stipulates that only residents of a Dutch municipality are allowed to enter coffeeshops.

As mentioned before in 1.2 this condition was introduced in the southern parts of the Netherlands to counter nuisance caused by tourists visiting Dutch coffeeshops. In January 2013 this condition was incorporated in the national directive and applied to coffeeshops throughout the country, even though not every part of the country is equally attractive for tourists, or if they have tourism, it does not necessarily mean they cause unacceptable nuisance or that there is a need to apply the I-condition. Other solutions to limit the nuisance are possible. By applying this condition to the entire country the local authorities are limited in their freedom to refrain from taking this measure because it is not necessary. The local authorities are very creative in finding a solution to evade this condition that is forced upon them. The minister of justice observed that in applying the I condition there is room for local variety.

---

[43] Article 108 section 1 of the Dutch law on municipals (Gemeentewet), in combination with art 120 and 212 of the same law.

[44] The local authorities can't deviate from the national policy or law. They also can't make rules about the same subject as the national law, unless the objective of the rule is different. Based on our law on municipals article 120 and 121. The directives are written for the prosecution and don't bind the local authorities officially, but de facto they will remain within the boundaries of the directives. Example given: A coffeeshop can have 500 grams of cannabis according to the national directive. A municipal can determine that the amount is lower than 500 grams. Officially they can also determine more is allowed but the person with more than 500 grams stash will be prosecuted in spite of the permission of the municipal.

Based on this remark the I-condition is mentioned in most local policies but is not enforced.

Another example of a complicating factor derives from the inconsistencies in the Dutch model. This complication surfaces in the interaction between the international and national level, but also in the interplay between the national and local level. Because the Dutch only allow the selling by coffeeshops and not the supplying of coffeeshops, they have created a loophole in the market where criminals can earn money and where there is no control on the quality of cannabis or on the cultivation of the product itself. If the energy used to grow cannabis is paid for, the energy company has a duty to report the high amount of used energy to the police who will then investigate whether cannabis is grown. Because of this rule the energy is often stolen, which can cause fire hazards. These problems (no quality control, drug tourism, organized crime taking over the market of growing cannabis, and fire hazards) can be solved in multiple ways. The Dutch tried to resolve it through criminal law enforcement which is cost-intensive and does not appear to be very effective in reducing the amount of cannabis that is grown. An alternative solution would be to regulate the growing of cannabis. 59 mayors have announced that they would like to regulate the growing of cannabis, in order to be able to solve the problems of fire hazards, caused by electricity, in order to be able to control the quality and to make the fight against organized crime more effective.[45]

The mayors that want to regulate the growth are precluded to do so because of national law. The current minister of justice made it very clear that he wouldn't be supportive of local initiatives that would allow the coffeeshops to cultivate cannabis enabling them to supply their own coffeeshops.[46]

1.5.2 Administrative and penal legislation

The national drugs policy has aspects of both administrative and penal law. The Dutch law on drugs is part of the criminal law system, but also contains administrative rules when it concerns the marihuana for medical purposes. The

[45] They signed a manifest called: Joint regulation, this was presented at the 31st of January 2014.

[46] Peter Oskam (politician for the Christian Democratic Party) even proposed a motion stating that the government should prevent the municipals to regulate the growing of cannabis. This motion was accepted by the government, 70 voted against and 75 voted in favor of the motion. *Kamerstukken II*, 2014-2015, 29 911, nr. 104. The minister confirms his view in a letter written 27th of May 2015: *Kamerstukken II*, 2014-2015, 24 077, nr. 346.

directive on the policy concerning coffeeshops is part of criminal law, as it is made by and addresses the public prosecution.

The local policy is made by the authorities of the municipality, the mayor, the counsel of mayor and aldermen, and the city council. It depends on the division in competence who is the most decisive in the local drugs policy, but usually it is the mayor.[47] This is part of the administrative law.

Criminal law and administrative law differ from each other in multiple ways. Each system consists of a different procedure containing different sanctions, means of enforcement, possibilities for a civilian to challenge sanctions or other decisions made by the public authority.

This juxtaposition of two areas of law is conducive of making the policy on drugs a complex one, basic knowledge of both fields of law is required to understand the policy. The rules are not conveniently placed together. Other complications arise when the fields of law are contradictory. In criminal law the principle of expediency implies that the public prosecution is at liberty to prosecute. In administrative law the principle on enforcement is different: If enforcement is possible it has to be done, unless there is an exception. Examples of such exceptions are that the behavior which is subject to administrative enforcement is reasonably expected to be lawful or that enforcement would be out of proportion in relation to the offence committed.[48]

When criminal and administrative law enforcement do not obviously collide, complications may arise when coordination is desirable but does not occur. As stated above, the local authorities have to stay within the limits of the national law when they are making rules. The directives offer additional guidance to the law, about when to prosecute in case of potential drug offences. As such they are

---

[47] I could write a paper about the competence of the different local authorities. Because cannabis is illegal, and the Dutch model is based on a directive simply addressing public prosecution not to prosecute under certain circumstances, the local authorities have no clear competence in making rules concerning drugs. They have to obey the national law stating it is prohibited. The directives do not address local administrative authorities directly. It is not possible under the law to give a permit to a coffeeshop because that would mean they act against the higher level of national law. It does happen in some municipality's, others get more creative by making additional rules to the law, or make drug policy rules that have different objective and can therefore still be seen as additional rules, some work with a 'toleration declaration' to avoid the permit, some tried to use the competence given to local authorities to act when public order is threatened. This explains why there are differences between municipality's in competence of the local authorities when it comes to making a local drug policy. More info on the different routes to local policy in my thesis: D. Bruin, *Onkruid vergaat niet*, Erasmus university Rotterdam 2012.

[48] ABRvS 30th June 2004, *Jurisprudentie Bestuursrecht* 2004, 293 (Haarlemse dakopbouw); ABRvS 4th of June 2014, ECLI:NL:RVS:2014:1982.

specifically directed at the public prosecution and not at the local authorities. Strictly speaking the local authorities are not directly obliged to take the directive into consideration. The only consequence of flouting the directive is that it might result in a criminal act by the person involved in drugs transactions. For example, if the mayor would allow a coffeeshop to have more than 500 grams of cannabis in the coffeeshop, then the public prosecution can prosecute the owner of the coffeeshop for committing a criminal offence. The prosecution of the local authorities is much more complicated because they have partial immunity when the criminal act is committed in the exercising of their public function.[49] Even though the local authorities are not directly affected by the directive, most of them follow the conditions from the directive in their own policy to avoid creating the possibility of others committing criminal acts. But it does go wrong occasionally. It did in the case that will serve as an example and will be discussed in the next paragraph (1.5.3).

Looking at the drug policy from the perspective of the public prosecution, they are not bound by local policy. If an act is conformity with the local rules or even encouraged by the local authorities, but is at the same time a criminal act because it does not comply with the directive, the public prosecutor can and will prosecute. Sometimes even without any deliberation with, or notification of, the local authorities. The complications that can arise from this construction will become clear in the next paragraph.

1.5.3 The Case of 'Checkpoint'

This case is named after the coffeeshop Checkpoint, which became one of the biggest coffeeshops in the Netherlands. This coffeeshop was situated near the border with Belgium in Terneuzen. Not only Dutch, but also Belgian, German and French customers visited the shop. The local authorities had close contact with the coffeeshop in their efforts to deal with drugdealers and drugrelated nuisances.[50] The mayor was aware of the size of the coffeeshop and did nothing to reduce the size, even though it must have been very clear that the amount of customers could not be sustained by the 500 grams cannabis that a coffeeshop is allowed to have. The mayor facilitated the growth of the coffeeshop by giving them a bigger parking lot when needed. Also the mayor had direction signs placed alongside the road, pointing to the coffeeshop. This measure was taken to prevent traffic nuisances caused by

---

[49] Hoge Raad (Supreme Court) 6th of January 1998, *Nederlandse Jurisprudentie* 1998, 367 with annotation JdH; Corstens/Borgers 2014, p. 194.

[50] The coffeeshop donated 1000 euros a month to help the local authorities in their fight against drug criminality.

drug tourists traveling by car, by directing them to the coffeeshop and therefore keeping them out of the city center. Although effective, it was a direct violation of the law on drugs which prohibits any advertising for cannabis. The violation was committed by the mayor in an attempt to solve a problem that was specific to his municipality.

Not only the mayor knew about the size of the coffeeshop. The tax agency knew as well. Based on the revenue, the agency should have known that this amount of revenue by one coffeeshop is only possible by having a stash of more than 500 grams cannabis.[51] The police checked the coffeeshop multiple times to figure out whether they acted in compliance with the rules of the directive. They would not enter certain areas of the building, or only check if the certain rules of the directive were observed.

In June 2007 the police entered the coffeeshop again for another check, but this time they did a very thorough investigation and large amounts of cannabis, 3777, 45 grams, were detected and confiscated. The owner and staff faced prosecution. The mayor followed suit by revoking the toleration declaration and closing the coffeeshop. This led to multiple court cases, in the realm of criminal law, administrative law and even private law, all related to the same event: possession of more than 500 grams cannabis.[52] Imagine the complexity of this case for the coffeeshop owner and staff, who had to prepare cases in three different areas of law. All this was the consequence of something that they had done for years and was generally known but had never been addressed by any authority. This can be seen as a consequence of the Dutch model, in which one act can lead to several cases within different areas of law and where a previously tolerated situation can be reassessed because one prosecutor suddenly decides to take action.

The differences between criminal law and administrative law come to the fore in the different outcomes of the cases. The criminal judge had to decide first if the decision to prosecute was in compliance with the principle of confidence. The administrative judge verified if the decision to revoke the toleration declaration and close the coffeeshop was in compliance with the principle of confidence. The administrative judges, the court of first instance and the court of appeal, all judged that the decision to close the coffeeshop was in compliance with the principle of confidence. Violation of the principle of confidence would be at stake if there was an affirmation or promise by a relevant authority, that the toleration declaration would not be

[51] This touches upon a complication I will not discuss further here. The tax agency wants to be able to collect tax from a coffeeshop, like a normal business. The problem is that the buying of cannabis is illegal and can't be made transparent to the tax agency. If the tax agency detects a criminal act they have to report it to the police.
[52] The latter concerned the labour law.

revoked in case of violation of the rules mentioned in the directive. The silent condoning, the limited checks by the police, and even the support of the mayor enabling the growth of the coffeeshop, were not sufficient to sustain a claim of trust. This judgement was to be expected as an appeal on the principle of confidence is rarely accepted. Especially not by the administrative judge who is very careful to respect the trias politica. The more freedom public authorities enjoy in making the decision, the more careful the judge will be in his assessment of their decision, in order to prevent their trespassing on the discretionary powers of the administrative authorities.

Although the judge within criminal law has more freedom to fully assess the decision, the outcome in first instance was the same as the administrative judge already had given: no violation of the principle of confidence. The fact that the authorities must have known about the violation but did not prosecute for a long time, is not enough to sustain the trust that the suspect was never going to be prosecuted for that violation. The court of appeal on the other hand did decide that the principle of confidence, among other principles, had been violated and that the prosecution therefore had lost its right to prosecute. This decision was overruled by the Supreme Court, which emphasized that the decision to declare that the prosecution lost its right to prosecute should only be applied in extraordinary situations and should be taken with great caution. The Supreme Court referred the verdict in this case to the court of appeal, who would have to make a new decision, taking the verdict of the Supreme Court into account. This verdict was given on the 16th of July 2014.[53] The court of appeal decided that the principle of confidence had been violated and that the prosecution therefore had partially lost its right to prosecute. The acts that they could still prosecute were pardoned, meaning they were proven and the suspect was found guilty but the judge did not impose any penalty. The Supreme Court overruled this decision again, and the verdict is once more referred to the court of appeal.[54]

The outcome of the administrative and criminal law cases so far has been quite different. Although the administrative decisions of closing the shop and revoking the toleration declaration, were only made because of the detection of criminal acts and the prosecution for those criminal acts, they remained in force after the criminal judge decided not to punish the criminal acts. This is in line with the Dutch system. The Una Via principle prevents double punishment of one act by means of administrative and criminal law. The decisions in this case made by the mayor, are not considered as punishment. By revoking the toleration declaration and closing the coffeeshop the mayor merely repaired an illegal situation. The administrative judge

[53] Hof Amsterdam (Court of appeal Amsterdam), 16th of July 2014, ECLI:NL: GHAMS:2014:2840.
[54] Hoge Raad (Supreme Court), 26th of May 2016, ECLI:NL:HR:2016:740.

and criminal judge gave their verdict over the different decisions made by different authorities, and they are not obliged to take each other's judgements into account when giving their own. That would be impossible and unnecessary, but when it comes to those issues of law where criminal and administrative law are so strongly intertwined, it can lead to complicated and sometimes even contradicting outcomes, that are only understandable with a solid knowledge of both criminal and administrative law. This is not contributing to a clear, transparent and accessible law.

2. Conclusion

In this essay the three levels and two major areas of law that determine the Dutch cannabis policy have been described. The different levels and areas, while adding to the complexity of the matter, have some advantages as well. By not determining the policy only at the national level, the Dutch legislator still leaves some room for the local authorities to adapt part of the policy to the specific needs of their municipality.

This chapter did not focus on the advantages, but only on the possible complications that may result from this layered structure. I want to stress that the layered structure does by definition make the drug policy more complex, in the sense that there is a lot of basic knowledge required to understand the entire policy at all levels and in all areas of law. This is a simple and unavoidable fact: the layered structure will make the policy more complex than it would be if all was arranged and coordinated at one level and in one field. Besides the complexity of the policy itself, the differences between levels and areas of law can be conducive of additional complexity of the policy. For example the ones mentioned in paragraph 1.4.2, 1.4.3 and 1.5.1. These latter complications are more specific to regions or situations and are not a necessary result of the layered structure as such. These specific complications can be avoided by more cooperation and synchronization between the different levels and fields of law. These specific complications can be further divided in complications specific to a region, specific to a situation, and complications that deteriorate the transparency of the policy on top of the general complexity that follows from the layered structure of the policy. An example of the latter can be the I-criteria described in par. 1.5.1. Because it is part of the national directive, it has a place in most local policies as well. But because the denial of access to coffeeshops of people that are no resident of a Dutch municipal is not a rule that is required in all municipalities, the rule is rarely enforced. Needless to say that it does not contribute to the transparency of the law and policy when the rules are written down locally, but only because the local authorities feel they should observe national policy and not because they are actually going to enforce those rules. This kind of unnecessary and misplaced politeness results in a token gesture that clouds the transparency even further. Another example would be the lip service the Dutch render to the SC, by criminalizing the possession and other acts concerning cannabis, but then systematically refraining from prosecuting those acts.

To what extent the general and specific complications can cause a problem or violation of principles is hard to say. The layered structure does not contribute to transparency in general. This might not be in direct violation of the principle of legality, demanding a clear and accessible description of the rules everyone in society is supposed to obey. But it surely does not contribute to the principle! The specific complications differ too much to allow any general statement . The coordination, or lack thereof, between criminal and administrative law does not directly violate any principle either . We have no principle spurring the government to act as one body towards civilians. I think this is however implied in the principle of legality. If the government is divided into different actors, they do not cooperate, take different decisions based on one act, or even oppose each other, then it becomes more difficult for a civilian to adjust his behavior to the law and policies.

The layered structure is not designed as a whole, but has developed piecemeal in different periods of history, by different representatives of different regions. The fields of criminal law and administrative law both have their own context and history as well. As understandable as this all may be, I think in a specific area of law, like the law concerning drugs, where the different levels and fields of law are so intertwined , the government, at all levels, should act more as one body making decisions. If different actors are involved in making one policy, this policy should function as a comprehensive system.

Bibliography

Bewley-Taylor 2012

D. Bewley-Taylor, *International Drug control: consensus fractured*, Cambridge: Cambridge University Press 2012.

Blom 1998

T. Blom, *Drugs in het recht, recht onder druk. Deel I : Ontwikkeling van de strafrechtelijke handhaving* (diss. Rotterdam), Arnhem: Gouda Quint 1998, (Dutch).

Blom 2015

T. Blom, *Opiumwetgeving en drugsbeleid*, Deventer: Kluwer 2015, (Dutch).

Bruin 2011

D. Bruin, *Onkruid vergaat niet. Ontwikkeling van het Nederlandse coffeeshopsbeleid en de samenwerking tussen strafrecht en bestuursrecht*, (masterthesis Erasmus University Rotterdam), Eindhoven: Organic Press 2011, (Dutch).

Buxton 2008

J. Buxton, *The historical foundations of the narcotic drug control regime*, World Bank Policy Research Working Paper 4553 (2008). Available online: < http://www-wds.worldbank.org >.

Van Kempen & Fedorova 2014

P.H.P.H.M.C. van Kempen & M.I. Fedorova, *Internationaal recht en cannabis. Een beoordeling op basis van VN-drugsverdragen en EU-drugsregelgeving van gemeentelijke en buitenlandse opvattingen pro regulering van cannabisteelt voor recreatief gebruik*, Deventer: Kluwer 2014.

Van Kempen & Fedorova 2016

P.H.P.H.M.C. van Kempen & M.I. Fedorova, *Internationaal recht en cannabis II, Regulering van cannabisteelt en -handel voor recreatief gebruik: positieve mensenrechtenverplichtingen versus VN-drugsverdragen*, Deventer: Kluwer 2016.

De Kort 1995

M. de Kort, *Tussen patiënt en delinquent. Geschiedenis van het Nederlandse drugsbeleid*, (diss. Rotterdam), Hilversum: Verloren 1995.

Musto 1987

D.F. Musto, *The American disease. Origins of narcotic control*, New York-Oxford: Oxford university press 1987.

Experts and the ultimate issue rule

Rolf Hoving [1]

1. Complex criminality and the use of experts

Criminality can be complex in many ways. One source of complexities may be the handling of the evidence that is needed to prove that an alleged crime really happened. Because of rapid technological and scientific developments it is getting more and more difficult for a lay fact finder to establish the facts. This is not only true with regard to complex criminal offences like drug-trafficking or money laundering, but also with regard to more straightforward criminal offences like theft. Due to the digital revolution, factual uncertainties concerning, for example, digital property lead to legal discussions concerning the definition of crimes. Advanced technology, like DNA-comparisons, GPS-tracking, facial recognition software and synthetic DNA-sprays add to or replace traditional ways of solving crime. And even questions that judges had to deal with for centuries, such as the reliability of witnesses, are nowadays subject to review by social scientists.

Because establishing facts in a criminal trial can be complex, it is common to call in experts. In a substantial number of cases, expert testimony forms the basis for the conviction. In the process of fact finding, the assistance of experts is needed, because the legal fact finder lacks the required knowledge to do this single-handedly. Although the use of expert evidence in a criminal trial is common and often needed, in many jurisdictions – inter alia, in the Netherlands and England and Wales (hereinafter England) – the precise responsibilities of the expert in a criminal procedure are not clear. Since the legal fact finder remains responsible for establishing the facts, the question arises how the fact finding responsibilities of the legal fact finder relate to the superior fact finding skills of the expert. This paper discusses the relationship between the fact finding responsibilities of legal fact finders (judges and juries) and experts. It therefore sets out to answer the question as to what the responsibilities of respectively the legal fact finder and the expert are in criminal procedure. In the next paragraph I will elaborate on this question from a theoretical perspective. In paragraph 3 and 4, I will describe the relationship between experts and legal fact finders in the English and Dutch criminal procedure.

---

[1] Mr. R.A. (Rolf) Hoving, PhD-candidate University of Groningen.

I will conclude with some observations based on a comparison of the relevant legal theory and the legal practice in England and the Netherlands.

2. Theory on fact finding in criminal trials

Generally speaking, the goal of a criminal trial is to determine whether the accused has committed a criminal offence. In order to reach this goal, the legal fact finder must first establish the facts of the case and subsequently apply the law to these established facts. The establishment of the facts is an essential task of a legal fact finder, whether this concerns a professional judge or a lay jury. Without establishing the facts, it is impossible to know the truth about what really happened; whether the accused indeed committed the alleged crime. But not all facts are relevant for a specific case. The law dictates what constitutes a crime. The law only attaches consequences to a specific set of facts. Only those facts have to be proven in a criminal trial. The facts to which the law attaches specified legal consequences are known as the constitutive facts of the case. When these facts are established, the accused may be convicted. Synonyms for constitutive facts are facts in issue, material facts or, in Dutch, *tenlastegelegde feiten*. Another synonym for facts to which the law attaches consequences is ultimate issues.[2] This term is of importance for this paper, because – as the title of the paper already indicates – in discussing the relationship between the responsibilities of the legal fact finder and the expert in the English and Dutch criminal trial, it will focus on the 'ultimate issue rule'.

The constitutive facts of a criminal case can be found in a (properly constructed) indictment which echoes the wording of a specific criminal offence. For example, s. 287 of the Dutch Criminal Code (CC) provides that a person commits manslaughter when he intentionally kills another person. An indictment tailored to manslaughter contains three ultimate issues: 1) another person is dead; 2) the accused killed this person; and 3) the accused acted intentionally.[3] It is noteworthy that offences contain several constitutive facts. Although the *final* question the fact finder in a criminal trial has to answer is whether the accused committed the crime, all constitutive facts of a crime need to be proven. Hence, all facts to which the law attaches consequences are ultimate issues.

Proof of the ultimate issues must be inferred from evidence. The use of evidence is necessary, because the legal fact finder was not present at the crime scene when the

---

[2] Roberts & Zuckerman 2010, p. 131.

[3] Other elements of the criminal liability in the Dutch criminal law system like guilt and unlawfulness are not mentioned in the wording of the provision.

alleged crime occurred. Two types of evidence may be recognized: i) oral and written testimony of witnesses and experts and ii) tangible evidence like objects, documents, video fragments and audio fragments.[4] Generally speaking, testimonies are the most important evidence for any (legal and non-legal) fact finder. To establish the occurrence of an event, the legal fact finder is always dependent on the testimony of persons who are in a position-to-know.[5] As in life in general, without testimonies it would be impossible to establish facts, especially where it concerns events that the fact finder did not experience himself consciously, ranging from his own date of birth to the eruption of a volcano.

In everyday life it is very common to trust the assertions of other people. Whether it is a newscaster, a teacher or a relative speaking about his or her day at work, we accept their statements as true because we believe they have knowledge about the topics they talk about. To put it in more epistemological terms, it is reasonable to trust people who are in a position-to-know[6] if one has good reasons to believe that the other person has good reasons to believe that a proposition is true.[7] In a criminal trial, witnesses and experts are persons in a position-to-know. Both witnesses and experts possess knowledge that legal fact finders do not have. They present their information to legal fact finders to enable them to discover what happened.

Despite the fact that witnesses and experts both provide information to the legal fact finder, they cannot be treated equally. There is a crucial distinction between the testimonies provided by witnesses and experts, which concerns the nature of the information they may provide. In a criminal trial the testimony of witnesses is relevant, because of the things they have seen, heard or done. Witnesses testify about situations where the legal fact finder was not present. In theory, practically everyone might have been capable of witnessing the events, but the witness coincidentally happened to be at the right place at the right time. Since most observations of witnesses are within the ordinary, the legal fact finder can autonomously infer from such testimony the most likely conclusions through the use of common sense generalisations and general background information. Because legal fact finders can make such inferences autonomously, witnesses are only permitted to state the 'facts'.[8]

Experts in a criminal procedure are allowed to testify about their opinions. Experts are persons who possess on a specific field of knowledge a certain level of

[4] Anderson, Schum & Twining 2005, p. 64.
[5] Walton 2006, p. 84.
[6] Walton 1997, p. 258. See par. 5.
[7] Hardwig 1985, p. 339.
[8] In practice, it is not possible to make the distinction between fact and opinion, because the 'facts' stated by witnesses are also the result of an inferences and therefore conclusions, see Roberts & Zuckerman 2010, p. 472.

knowledge and skills which is i) higher than the knowledge and skills of their public and ii) sufficient to perform the tasks of the expert (the provision of information and advice to their public) in an adequate manner.[9] Expert opinions are necessary, because the legal fact finder does not have enough knowledge and skills to make sense of some of their own observations or the observations provided by witnesses. For example, a criminal investigation officer says that he, as a witness, saw a drop of blood. This testimony is by itself useless. The legal fact finder needs someone who can infer useful conclusions from this observation. An expert in DNA-comparison is capable of extracting useful information from the drop of blood which is found at the crime scene by extracting the DNA from the blood and by comparting this DNA with the DNA of the accused. Because the legal fact finder needs the conclusions of the expert, experts are in a criminal trial allowed to testify to their 'opinions'.

Because the expert draws conclusions the legal fact finder is not able to draw himself, it is possible that the expert can and must testify to the existence of facts which (almost or exactly) coincide with the ultimate issues. This is especially the case if the legal norms contain terms of which the factual existence can only be established by an expert. In the Netherlands, examples thereof can be found in the *Opiumwet* (Opium Act), the *Wet wapens en munitie* (Weapons and Ammunition Act) or the *Wet economische delicten* (Economic Offences Act). In the *Opiumwet*, the existence of prohibited drugs forms an essential part of the definition of the criminal offence while some of these drugs can only be identified by an expert. With regard to the *Wet wapens en munitie*, it is often only an expert who can identify to which category of prohibited or non-prohibited weapons the weapon in question belongs. The *Wet economische delicten* covers a variety of economic and environmental offences substantiated in specific acts. Because of the technical nature of such offences, often only experts are able to establish whether the defendant has breached the law. These are therefore examples of the close relationship between complex criminal legal norms and the establishment of the underlying facts.

Witnesses and legal fact finders may possess the same kind of general knowledge and skills, but the legal fact finders are laymen where it concerns the field of knowledge of an expert. Because of the difference in knowledge and skills between experts and legal fact finders, legal fact finders are not able to assess the reliability of the inferences made by the expert. This is known as the 'novice-expert' problem.[10] In a criminal trial, there is a tension between the inability of the legal fact

[9] The definition of an expert is taken from Hoving 2015. This definition of an expert encompasses forensic criminal investigation officers as well, who are – at least in the Netherlands – formally no expert.
[10] Goldman, 2001, p. 22. The problem becomes magnified when there are more experts who contradict each other: the 'novice/2-expert problem'.

finder to assess the reliability of the expert testimony and the responsibility of the legal fact finder to establish the facts. This is known in the Netherlands as the paradox of experts.[11]

The tension between the responsibilities of legal fact finders and their epistemological capacities are most pressing when it comes to ultimate issues. Because the legal fact finders are responsible for establishing the facts, it is not clear whether experts are allowed to make factual assertions about the ultimate issues. The position and responsibilities of the legal fact finder can be regarded as under threat if the expert would be allowed to testify about the ultimate issue. A solution for this problem is to protect the responsibility of the legal fact finders by prohibiting the expert to make assertions regarding the ultimate issues: this is known as 'the ultimate issue rule'.

In theory, the ultimate issue rule prohibits both witnesses and experts to testify about ultimate issues. However, for witnesses this follows already from the rule that they are only allowed to state 'facts' (observations) and not to talk about their opinions and conclusions. Hence, in practice the ultimate issue rule is only relevant to experts. The ultimate issue rule does not distinguish between the several ultimate issues of an offence. It applies both to more 'factual' ultimate issues – for example, whether the victim is dead – and more 'normative' ultimate issues – for example, whether the accused acted intentionally. In defending the ultimate issue rule, most advocates focus on the 'normative' ultimate issues. They claim, for example, that the expert is not allowed to testify about the intentions of the accused, because the establishment of the intentions of the accused in a criminal trial is directly linked to an opinion about the culpability of the acts of the accused. But the rule's advocates do not restrict the rule's application to 'normative' ultimate issues, nor does such a limitation of its application follow from the rule itself. Therefore, the ultimate issue rule prohibits experts to make statements about all ultimate issues.

3. The ultimate issue rule in England

In England, the jury is the legal fact finder that is responsible for the establishment of the facts. The jury may use expert evidence as a basis for its decision. Experts must 'help the court to achieve' that criminal cases being dealt with justly 'by giving objective, unbiased opinion on matters within his expertise' (r.1.1 and r. 19.2(1) Criminal Procedure Rules). Traditionally, the idea was that a jury should be capable of deciding on the facts after being educated by the expert. After being educated, the

[11] Van Koppen 2004, p. 6.

jury should be able to understand the way in which the expert reached his conclusions and to independently assess the inferences made by the expert. This idea was explicated in Davie v. Edinburgh Magistrates:

'*Their duty* [of the experts, RH] *is to furnish the judge or jury with the necessary scientific criteria for testing the accuracy of their conclusions, so as to enable the judge or jury to form their own independent judgment by the application of these criteria to the facts proved in evidence.*'[12]

However, in actual practice the jury almost always defers to the conclusions of the expert. Educating laymen is indeed the ideal solution for the 'novice-expert problem', but it proofs to be untenable. It is impossible to teach the jury sufficiently about all the fields of knowledge that experts may testify about. Even in relation to one field of knowledge, it may proof very difficult to educate all the members of the jury up to such a level as to enable them to fully comprehend the expert testimony and in order for them to be able to evaluate the conclusions of the expert. In the unlikely situation that it were possible to teach jurors sufficiently about things like DNA-comparison or psychological research, such education would require far more time and resources than available in a criminal trial.[13] The jury, therefore, has no choice but to defer to the expert.

As a consequence of this deference by the jury to the expert, the question arose whether the expert could testify to the ultimate issues the jury has to decide upon. An old common law rule from the 19th century prohibited this.[14] According to that rule, a witness (either expert or non-expert) should not express an opinion on those issues that should be determined by the court.[15] Roberts and Zuckerman state about this rule that 'the animating notion is that no expert witness, no matter how knowledgeable or eminent, should be allowed to express a conclusion on the very facts at issue – the ''ultimate'' issue(s) – in the trial which the jury is being called upon to resolve'.[16] Whether the expert indeed testifies to the ultimate issues had to be assessed by the trial judge when determining the admissibility of the evidence. The trial judge could deem the expert evidence inadmissible because of, for example, the lack of reliability of his testimony. In assessing the admissibility of the expert evidence, the trial judge could further take into account whether the expert made statements about the ultimate issues. If this was the case, the trial judge could refuse to allow the expert to make the statement in question in front of the jury.

---

[12] Davie v Edinburgh Magistrates [1953] SC 34, 40.
[13] Roberts & Zuckerman, p. 474.
[14] Archbold 2014, chapter 10-51 refer to R. v. Wright (1821) Russ. & Ry. 456. But according to Roberts & Zuckerman 2010, p. 491 it is doubtful whether any such rule ever fully been recognized.
[15] Blackstone 2013, F10.34.
[16] Roberts & Zuckerman 2010, p. 490.

Nowadays, the ultimate issue rule no longer has standing in common law. Already in 1972 the Law Commission concluded that the rule no longer existed.[17] More recently, the Court of Appeal in R v Atkins also denied the existence of this rule, stating that:[18]

The rejection of this second submission was chiefly couched, as plainly the argument had been, in terms of what used sometimes to be described as the "ultimate issue" question, viz: is there a rule that the witness cannot give his opinion on the very question the jury must answer? (There is not: consider for example insanity ...)

Before the ruling in Atkins the ultimate issue rule was largely ignored in English criminal trials. This becomes clear from the case R v Stockwell, where it was held that:[19]

'The rationale behind the supposed prohibition is that the expert should not usurp the functions of the jury. But since counsel can bring the witness so close to opining on the ultimate issue that the inference as to his view is obvious, the rule can only be (...) a matter of form rather than substance. In our view an expert is called to give his opinion and he should be allowed to do so.'

The Court of Appeal pointed out that it is difficult to differentiate between the ultimate issues and the intermediate facts from which the ultimate issues can be inferred, because the last inference can be really totally obvious. This can be illustrated by an example. The simple testimony of a pathologist that the victim was cold and did not breathe, is strictly speaking different from the ultimate issue whether the victim is dead. But the inference is so obvious, that it would have not made any difference if the pathologist would instead have said that the victim was dead.

The expert in English criminal proceedings is allowed to state his opinions about the ultimate issues. The question must be asked how this can be reconciled with the fact finding responsibilities of a jury. The answer to this question starts with the establishment of the fact that when confronted with expert testimony, a jury is not obliged to accept everything the expert says. The jury can choose to accept or reject the expert testimony, without having to give reasons for its decision. Even reliable expert evidence may be rejected by the jury. The trial judge is not permitted to instruct a jury that it must rely on the expert findings.[20] Instead the judge 'should

[17] Criminal Law Revision Committee 1972, par. 268, cited from Blackstone 2013, F10.34.
[18] R v Atkins [2009] EWCA Crim 1876, [14].
[19] R v Stockwell [1993] 97 Cr App R 260, CA.
[20] R v Flynn and St John [2008] 2 Cr App R 20.

make clear to the jury that they are not bound by the expert's opinion, and that the issue is for them to decide'.[21]

The jury retains its fact finding responsibilities, because of its power to accept or reject all expert evidence as it sees fit. But the unreasoned acceptance or rejection of all expert evidence by the jury is not the ideal solution for the problem of the tension between the responsibilities of legal fact finder and the knowledge of the expert. It endangers the rationality of the fact finding, while rationality is one of the basic assumptions of reasonable fact finding in a criminal trial. Acceptance or dismissal can be based on 'irrelevant considerations, like the eloquence or charisma of a particular expert witness, and prejudicial grounds for accepting or rejecting testimony, such as a juror's personal animus or lack of comprehension'.[22] The choice of a jury between deference to or rejection of expert testimony should be based on rational grounds.

4. The ultimate issue rule in the Netherlands

In the Netherlands, the legal fact finder is a professional judge. There are some differences between the rules of evidence in the Netherlands and England. Unlike England, the admissibility of the evidence is not regulated in the Dutch Code of Criminal Procedure (CPC). The fact finder is permitted to see all proffered evidence. Instead of admissibility rules, the CPC contains rules regarding the evidence that judges may use in his judgement (s. 338-344a CPC) and regarding the duty of judges to give reasons for their decisions (s. 358-359 CPC). Judges are permitted to use expert testimony in which an opinion is given about topics within the expert's field of knowledge (s. 343 and 344 par. 1 under 4 CPC). If a judge rules that the accused committed the crime he has to sum up the evidence he used in arriving at his decision, including the used expert testimony (s. 359 par. 3 CPC). However, a judge is not obliged to explain why he used particular evidence. Decisions relating to the selection and assessment of evidence fall within the judge's discretionary powers.[23]

As a consequence of the non-existence of admissibility rules and the judges' discretionary powers to select and assess the evidence, there appear to be no legal

[21] R v Stockwell [1993] 97 Cr App R 260, CA, p. 266. The consequence of this is that the jury may accept or reject the expert testimony on irrational grounds. The very interesting questions how to rationalize this decision making process lays, unfortunately, beyond the scope of this paper.
[22] Roberts & Zuckerman 2010, p. 474.
[23] Corstens/Borgers 2014, p. 848.

limitations as to the content of expert testimony. As long as the testimony's content falls within the expert's field of knowledge, any statement can be used.[24] However, several Dutch authors state that there do exist limitations as to what an expert may testify about. This point of view is based on an idea regarding the respective roles of the judge and the expert as well as on a particular interpretation of several decisions of the Dutch Supreme Court. According to Nijboer, one of these authors, expert testimony may not '*anticipate upon judgements which are reserved for the judge and may also not contain decisions that the judge is charged with to make*'.[25] The judgement that is reserved for the judge (*voorbehouden oordeel*) is seen by them as the Dutch version of the ultimate issue rule.[26]

An ultimate issue rule is argued to exist in the Netherlands by the advocates of the ultimate issue rule, firstly, by pointing to the legal principle that the respective roles of judges and experts must be strictly separated. Making decisions in a criminal trial is the sole responsibility of the judge. The answering of questions like whether the accused committed an offence, whether the offender's acts were unlawful, whether the offender acted blameworthy and which punishment the offender deserves, are all reserved for the judge.[27] As a fact finder, the judge also has to decide whether the constitutive facts of the offence in question are proven. The only duty of the expert is to provide information or to do research (s. 51i par. 1 CPC). From the foregoing widely accepted premises it can be inferred that the expert is not permitted to make statements about the ultimate issues (or reserved judgements). This, however, would be a strange inference. Statements of an expert about the ultimate issues are not binding on the judge. The judge is free to accept or reject the testimony of an expert. In some cases, the judge may have to give reasons for such a decision, for example, when objections are raised concerning the reliability of the expert.[28] But such a duty to give reasons does not alter the fact that the judge has the power to make the decision. Therefore, the decision-making power lies with the judge even if the expert testifies to the ultimate issues.

---

[24] In Corstens/Borgers 2014 and Keulen & Knigge 2010 the subject is not explicitly discussed. Keulen & Knigge do discuss the conclusions a witness is allowed to make and whether the judge can use this testimony. According to Keulen & Knigge, p. 494 it is not allowed for the judge to rely on the witness too much.

[25] Nijboer 2011, p. 198 '*vooruit (...) lopen op het aan de rechter voorbehouden oordeel en daarnaast geen aan de rechter opgedragen beslissingen mag bevatten*'. See also Borst 1985, p. 258; Hielkema 1996, p. 213; Malsch 2001, p. 189; comments Dubelaar to s. 342 and 343 CPC in *T&C Strafvordering*; comment 10 Van Kampen to s. 343 CPC in Melai/Groenhuijsen. Van Koppen is more accommodating in: Van Koppen 2004, p. 34.

[26] Nijboer 2011, p. 198.

[27] Borst 1985, p. 258.

[28] Hoge Raad (Supreme Court) 27th of January 1998, *Nederlandse Jurisprudentie* 1998, 404 m.nt. J.M. Reintjes.

Secondly, the existence of an ultimate issue rule in Dutch criminal procedure is argued by the advocates of the ultimate issue rule by referring to the case law of the Dutch Supreme Court. There are two categories of cases these advocates refer to: cases about witnesses and cases about judgements reserved for the judge.

The first category of cases is about witnesses. The Supreme Court decided repeatedly that a witness is not permitted to state their conclusions (in general, not only as regards the ultimate issues). It held, for example, that a witness is not permitted to testify as to the conclusion that the accused was not able to drive his car because he was drunk.[29] This prohibition also applies to criminal investigation officers (they form a special category of witnesses but are regarded as witnesses nonetheless). In a similar vein, criminal investigation officers are not permitted to state their conclusions, for example, that the accused was 'a keeper of doves',[30] that 'certain pictures contained child pornography' (at least not without describing these pictures),[31] or that 'a car with a broken v-belt is still controllable'.[32]

The advocates of the ultimate issue rule make a comparison between the testimonies of witnesses and those of experts. Because witnesses are not permitted to testify about ultimate issues, this should also apply to experts. But this reasoning is flawed. As follows from s. 342 CPC, witnesses are not allowed to make a statement that contains a conclusion and may only testify to the facts, *i.e.*, to things the witness has seen, heard or experienced.[33] Experts, however, are explicitly allowed to state their opinions, to report their observations and the conclusions they infer from these observations (s. 343 CPC). According to advocates of an ultimate issue rule, an expert's testimony cannot contain conclusions about ultimate issues, because a witnesses' testimony is not permitted to contain conclusions. This reasoning does not pay any regard to the distinctions between witnesses and experts and is therefore incomprehensible.

The second category of cases the advocates of the ultimate issue rule use in their argument is about judgements reserved for the judge. In two cases the Supreme Court, quashed decisions by the Court of Appeal because the testimony of the expert

---

[29] Hoge Raad (Supreme Court) 8th of May 1933, *Nederlandse Jurisprudentie* 1933, p. 1102.
[30] Hoge Raad (Supreme Court) 15th of November 2005, ECLI:NL:HR:2005:AU2711. In s. 37 Gezondheids- en welzijnswet voor dieren one of the constitutive facts is 'keeper of animals' (*houder van dieren*).
[31] Hoge Raad (Supreme Court) 1st of July 2008, *Nederlandse Jurisprudentie* 2008, 454. In s. 240b Wetboek van Strafrecht one of the constitutive facts is 'a picture of a sexual act, with which a person who apparently has not reached the age of eighteen years, is involved' (*een afbeelding (...) van een seksuele gedraging, waarbij iemand die kennelijk de leeftijd van achttien jaar nog niet heeft bereikt, is betrokken*).
[32] Hoge Raad (Supreme Court) 29th of March 2011, *Jurisprudentie in Nederland* 2011, 399.
[33] The blurry boundaries between facts and opinions, and the case law of the Supreme Court with regard to this, are described in Keulen & Knigge 2010, p. 492.

contained statements about a judgement that was reserved for the judge. In the first case, the expert, a criminal investigation officer, made statements about the interpretation of a working conditions regulation.[34] The Court of Appeal used the testimony of the expert without explaining why this interpretation of the regulation was correct. According to the Supreme Court, the statement of the expert concerned a judgement that was reserved for the judge to make. The Court of Appeal would have been permitted to use the testimony of the expert, but not without giving reasons. Because such reasons were missing, the case was remitted to the Court of Appeal. The rationale of this ruling is that the judge is reckoned to be an expert in law. Because of the judge's expertise, he may not simply defer to legal conclusions in the testimony of an external expert. There is no insurmountable gap of knowledge. The judge can look into the reliability of the contents of the expert evidence and test whether the statements are justified. A judge is permitted to listen to external experts testifying to the law, but not to defer to those experts without giving reasons. Aside from this constraint, there appears to exist no ultimate issue rule with regards to experts testifying to the interpretation of law.

The second case offers – at least at first sight – a more convincing argument that the ultimate issue rule exists in Netherlands. In Hoge Raad 21st of November 2000, *Nederlandse Jurisprudentie* 2001, 48 the Supreme Court allowed the appeal and remitted the case to the Court of Appeal, because the testimony of the expert contained a statement which was a reserved judgement. The accused – a transport company – was convicted for transporting a pig while this pig was more than lightly wounded, thereby causing unnecessary suffering to the pig.[35] The conviction was based solely on the testimony of the expert, who was a veterinary surgeon. The expert had been employed by the government to inspect slaughterhouses. The expert reported that he had seen a pig that was more than lightly wounded, which was a constitutive fact (and therefore an ultimate issue) of the offence. He described several defects of the pig, such as malnourishment, brain damage and a crippled leg. The expert also reported the name of the owner of the pig and the fact that the pig was transported by the defendant.

[34] Hoge Raad (Supreme Court) 18th of May 1993, *Nederlandse Jurisprudentie* 1993, 782. See also Rechtbank Haarlem (Court of First Instance), 27th of March 1930, *Nederlandse Jurisprudentie* 1930, p. 1131.

[35] This offence is an example of the complex and layered nature of economic offences. Until 2007 the obligation to not transport wounded animals could be found in s. 5 of Besluit dierenvervoer 1994. This delegated legislation was made because s. 60 of the Gezondheids- en welzijnswet voor dieren required this. The breach of the in accordance with s. 60 Gezondheids- en welzijnswet voor dieren formulated Besluit was according to s.1 par. 1 under 4 Wet economische delicten an offence which according to s. 2 par. 4 jo. s. 6 par. 1 under 4 Wet economische delicten was punishable.

On appeal, the defence did not object to the fact that the expert had testified about the ultimate issues. Instead, the defence argued that the conviction was not valid, because it was based on the sole testimony of the expert, who was not an official criminal investigator. This defence concerned the minimum amount of evidence that is required in order to convict an accused under Dutch law. The Dutch law does not allow convictions based the testimony of a single witness (s. 342 par. 2 CPC). However, the judge is explicitly permitted to base a conviction on the single written testimony (*proces-verbaal*) of a criminal investigator (s. 344 par. 2 CPC), which is attributed a special status.

Whether a conviction may be based on the testimony of a single expert is not clear, because (unlike criminal investigators) the expert is not a witness under Dutch law. From the precise wording of the provisions regarding expert testimony (s. 343 and s. 344 par. 1 under 4 CPC), it does not directly follow that there should be more than one expert testimony in order to be able to arrive at a conviction. Nijboer argues that, with the exception of criminal investigation officers, there should always be a second source of evidence,[36] but such a rule does not seem to be part of Dutch law.[37] Borst is convinced that in actual practice a single testimony of an expert can never provide enough proof in order to arrive at a conviction.[38] Jörg agrees with Borst and argues that a conviction which is based on a single expert testimony is merely a theoretical possibility and therefore of no practical relevance.[39]

The case of the veterinary surgeon illustrates that it is very difficult to base a conviction solely on the testimony of a single expert. The expert made a statement about two distinct topics: the wellbeing of the pig and the identity of the transport company. The first statement is well within the field of knowledge of a veterinary surgeon: animal sickness and animal suffering. The second statement concerning the identity of the transport company is not within the field of veterinary knowledge. A veterinary is not specifically trained to identify transport companies. In such a matter, he possesses just about as much knowledge as the average person. Such a statement must be qualified as a statement of an ordinary witness. The distinction between the two types of statements was made by the Supreme Court. The (appeals) judges could have used the statements of the expert about the wellbeing of the pig, including the conclusion concerning the ultimate issue that the pig was more than lightly wounded. But identifying the transport company went beyond the expert's

---

[36] Nijboer 2011, p. 76.
[37] See the advice of A-G Jörg in Hoge Raad (Supreme Court) 21st of November 2000, *Nederlandse Jurisprudentie* 2001, 48. Jörg was the Advocate-General in this case. In the Netherlands the Advocate-General is an independent adviser who provides the Supreme Court in each case with an authoritative advice.
[38] Borst 1985, p. 31.
[39] Hoge Raad (Supreme Court) 21st of November 2000, *Nederlandse Jurisprudentie* 2001, 48, advice A-G Jörg par. 7-10.

expertise, which rendered it a witness statement. As said, Dutch law does not allow that an accused is convicted on the basis of a testimony of a single witness. In this case there was no other evidence available to link the transport company to the transport. Therefore, the courts in first instance and on appeal should not have based their decisions solely on the part of the testimony of the veterinary surgeon which contained witness statements. The Supreme Court held that: '*In as much as the aforementioned statement also includes that the inspected pig was transported by H.G.B. from Huissen, this statement contains a conclusion drawn by the veterinary surgeon that is reserved for the judge to make.*'[40]

The ruling of the Supreme Court is expressed in the – somewhat awkward – wording that the conclusion by the expert had to be regarded as a conclusion reserved for the judge to make. On the basis of a close reading of the preceding part of the judgement, however, it becomes clear that the Supreme Court's reasoning does not entail an argument for the existence of an ultimate issue rule in the Netherlands. To the contrary, the Supreme Court explicitly states that the expert could testify to the conclusion that the pig was more than lightly wounded,[41] while this is an ultimate issue. The expert may testify to the ultimate issues, as long as those issues are within the field of knowledge of the expert. Moreover, and hypothetically speaking, the judge may probably even base his decision on a single testimony of a single expert, containing conclusions about ultimate issues.

This viewpoint can be corroborated with the judgment in a recent other case. In: Hoge Raad (Supreme Court), 3rd of September 2013, *Rechtspraak van de Week* 2013, 1043, the accused had been convicted by de court of appeal for committing several offences constituting the abuse of animals. One of the offences concerned the abuse of two horses. The court of appeal had based its conviction on the reports of an expert: (again) a veterinary surgeon. On appeal, the accused complained that the judge should not have used the conclusion of the expert that the horses had been withheld the necessary care, since 'withholding of necessary care' constituted an ultimate issue.[42] According to the defence, this qualified as an opinion of the expert about a subject that belonged to the reserved judgement of the judge. The Supreme

---

[40] Hoge Raad (Supreme Court) 21st of November 2000, *Nederlandse Jurisprudentie* 2001, 48, r.o. 3.6. '*Voorzover voormelde verklaring tevens inhoudt dat het onderzochte varken was aangevoerd door H.G. B. te Huissen, behelst zij een conclusie van de keuringsarts die aan de rechter is voorbehouden.*'

[41] Hoge Raad (Supreme Court) 21st of November 2000, *Nederlandse Jurisprudentie* 2001, 48, r.o. 3.5. '*Gelet hierop kan uit voormelde verklaring slechts worden afgeleid dat het door de deskundige onderzocht varken " ziek en/of gewond was (met de symptomen kyphose, zeer mager, arthritis rechtsachter) terwijl het betrof een meer dan licht ziek en/of meer dan licht gewond dier, waarvoor het vervoer onnodig lijden tot gevolg had", zoals is bewezenverklaard*'.

[42] See s. 37 Gezondheids- en welzijnswet voor dieren, 'de nodige verzorging te onthouden'.

Court did not discuss this complaint by the defence, since answering it would not contribute to the development of the law. In his advice to the Supreme Court, however, Machielse did not agree with the defence's reasoning. In his opinion, the conclusion of the expert contained knowledge that is very common.

Inferring from the above that the Supreme Court allows an expert to testify to ultimate issues, may explain another recent judgement of the Supreme Court. In *HR 19 november 2013, Nederlandse Jurisprudentie 2014, 39*, the accused had been convicted on appeal for the possession of an air gun that strongly resembled a bullet gun due its shape, size and colour (s. 2 par 1 under 7 *Wet wapens en munitie*). The gun had been ordered abroad on internet and had been intercepted at the airport during shipment. The court of appeal's finding as to the resemblance was based on the testimony of a criminal investigation officer. The defence objected against the conclusion drawn by the criminal investigation officer that the gun belonged to a prohibited category of weapons. The defence argued that the gun was not prohibited in the Netherlands, because it could be bought in regular businesses. After consultation, the prosecutor agreed and asked for an acquittal. But the court of appeal convicted the accused nonetheless. The Supreme Court dismissed the appeal, pointing to the fact that the criminal investigation officer was a gun expert.[43] The Supreme Court took the expertise of the expert as a given, because the defence did not raise any objections thereto. As an expert, the criminal investigation officer was permitted to make a statement about topics within his field of knowledge such as gun resemblance, notwithstanding the fact that the testimony of the gun expert concerned the main ultimate issue of the definition of the offence. Although Machielse, in his advise to the Supreme Court, was of the opinion that the first instance and appeals judges should have made their own assessments of the testimony of the gun expert, the Supreme Court did consider the absence of such assessment problematic.

[43] There is much to be said about the expert status of criminal investigation officers, but I will not go into this. In his comment Borgers pointed out that if the High Court indeed labeled the criminal investigation officer as an expert, the process of appointment and swearing in was faulty. Therefore he concludes that the High Court could not have seen the criminal investigation officer as expert. My conclusion is that the High Court did see the criminal investigation officer as expert, and that the High Court turns a blind eye to the faults in the formal procedure of appointing an expert.

5. Conclusion: the need for a critical assessment of expert testimony

In both England and the Netherlands, there appear to exist no limitations for experts to make statements regarding ultimate issues. There exists no ultimate issue rule in England as it was held explicitly by the Court of Appeal in R. v Atkins. Also in the Netherlands, there exists no ultimate issue rule. The law of Dutch criminal procedure does not provide any ground for arguing that there exist limitations as to the content of expert testimony, except that the expert has to limit his testimony to the field of his knowledge. Several Dutch authors argue that an ultimate issue rule exists on the basis of the distinct roles of judges and experts in a criminal trial and on the basis of the case-law of the Supreme Court. After careful consideration of their arguments, however, their arguments do not seem valid. Instead, it follows from the Supreme Court's case law that experts are permitted to testify about ultimate issues.

The discussion about whether an ultimate issue rule exists must be seen against the background of the bigger issue concerning the fact finding responsibilities of the legal fact finder. Because of the gap of knowledge between fact finders and experts, the fact finder is not able to autonomously assess the reliability of the contents of the experts' reports. The ultimate issue rule tries to shield the fact finding responsibilities of the legal fact finder from unwanted influence by external experts. From a formal viewpoint this is not necessary, since the legal fact finder is not obliged to believe or use the testimony of the expert. Only the legal fact finder is entitled to establish the facts in a criminal trial. Fact finding remains the responsibility of the legal fact finder, whether the expert testifies about ultimate issues or not. Therefore, the absence of an ultimate issue rule does not formally infringe upon the powers of the legal fact finder.

Advocates of the ultimate issue rule are trying to solve a problem that does not exist. The problem is not whether the legal fact finder is entitled to choose whether or not to believe and make use of the expert testimony, but whether the legal fact finder is capable of doing this. The ultimate issue rule does not take away the gap of knowledge between legal fact finders and experts. Even when the expert does not testify to ultimate issues, the legal fact finder still has to evaluate his testimony. Such evaluation must be done in a rational manner. Conclusions of an expert should be regarded critically, whether they concern ultimate issues or not. An ultimate issue rule cannot make the decision process more rational. The problem can only be resolved by enabling legal fact finders to critically assess the testimony of the expert. Therefore, a framework for assessing the value of expert opinions should be developed in order to enable the legal fact finder to exercise his fact finding responsibilities in a sound way. A framework for assessing expert opinions is crucial in a society that is rapidly changing and in which complex legal norms are established to keep such developments in track. The use of experts is essential and inevitable in coping with complex criminality. Limiting the substantive scope of expert testimony is not the right approach for handling the knowledge gap. The dependency on expert testimony is not taken away by reinforcing the power of the legal fact finder with a formal ultimate issue rule. Instead, legal fact finders should be instructed about how they can assess expert testimony. Legal fact finders should become experts in fact finding and experts in assessing expert testimony. This should be the preferred approach regarding the role of the expert in complex (and less complex) criminality.

Bibliography

Anderson, Schum & Twining 2005

T. Anderson, D. Schum & W. Twining, *Analysis of evidence*, (2nd edition), Cambridge: Cambridge University Press 2005.

Archbold

P.J. Richardson (ed.), *Archbold. Criminal pleading, evidence and practice*, digital edition.

Blackstone 2013

P. Murphy (red.), *Blackstone's Criminal Practice 2013*, (21st edition), Oxford: Oxford University Press 2012.

Borst 1985

W.L. Borst, *De bewijsmiddelen in strafzaken*, Arnhem: Gouda Quint 1985.

Corstens/Borgers 2014

G.J.M. Corstens, *Het Nederlandse strafprocesrecht,* bewerkt door M.J. Borgers, Deventer: Kluwer 2011.

Criminal Law Revision Committee 1972

Criminal Law Revision Committee, *Eleventh Report: Evidence (General)* 1972.

Goldman 2001

A.I. Goldman, 'Experts which ones should you trust?', *Philosophy and Phenomenological Research* 2001, 63, p. 85-109.

Hardwig 1985

J. Hardwig, 'Epistemic Dependence', *The Journal of Philosophy* 1985, 82, p. 335-349.

Hielkema 1996

J. Hielkema, *Deskundigen in Nederlandse strafzaken* (diss. Rotterdam), 's-Gravenhage: Sdu Juridische & Fiscale Uitgeverij 1996.

Hoving 2015

R.A. Hoving, 'Wat is een deskundige? Over het deskundigenbegrip binnen en buiten het (strafproces)recht', *RM Themis* 2015, 2, p. 43-56.

Keulen & Knigge 2010

B.F. Keulen & G. Knigge, *Strafprocesrecht*, Deventer: Kluwer 2010.

Van Koppen 2004

P.J. van Koppen, *Paradoxen van deskundigen. Over de rol van experts in strafzaken* (diss. Maastricht), Deventer: Kluwer 2004.

Malsch 2001

M. Malsch, 'De stoel van de jurist', in: P.B Cliteur e.a. (eds.), *It ain't necessaraly so* (Franken-bundel), Leiden: E.M. Meijers Instituut 2001.

Melai/Groenhuijsen

A.L. Melai, *Het wetboek van strafvordering* (voortgezet onder redactie van M.S. Groenhuijsen); digital edition.

Nijboer 2011

J.F. Nijboer, *Strafrechtelijk bewijsrecht*, (6[e] druk), Nijmegen: Ars Aequi Libri 2011.

Roberts & Zuckerman 2010

P. Roberts & A. Zuckerman, *Criminal evidence* (2e druk), Oxford: Oxford University Press 2010.

T&C Strafvordering

C.P.M. Cleiren & M.J.M. Verpalen (eds.), *Strafvordering: de tekst van het Wetboek van Strafvordering en enkele aanverwante wetten voorzien van commentaar (*Reeks Tekst & Commentaar 9e druk*)*, digital edition.

Walton 1997

D. Walton, *Appeal to Expert Opinion. Arguments from Authority*, Pennsylvania: The Pennsylvania State University Press 1997.

Walton 2006

D. Walton, *Fundamentals of Critical Argumentation*, Cambridge: Cambridge University Press 2006.

Maintain Proportionate Sentencing in Rewarding Criminal Cooperators

Wei Pei[1]

Introduction

Criminal justice authorities in China and England and Wales are exploring effective approaches to solving crimes. A strategy adopted in common is to encourage the accused person to provide assistance during the investigation or prosecution of other crimes or the conviction of other suspects. To facilitate such cooperation, in recent years both jurisdictions have developed legal rules that allows or even encourages a mutually-beneficial exchange between the offender's assistance , either by providing information to investigators as an informant or 'whistle blower' or by giving testimony in court as a special witness, and legal concessions from criminal justice authorities.

These rules are designed to enhance the detection of crimes. However, they also raise questions especially as how and to what extent the offenders' assistance shall be rewarded. Behind these questions lies an even fundamental one , that is how to define and measure a proper and reasonable sanction. Academia has been tirelessly working on this subject,[2] and competing rationales, especially the 'desert model' and the consequentialist's ideas such as incapacitation, rehabilitation and deterrence, have been developed.[3] Generally the key question here is not whether multiple considerations exist in sentencing, but which group has the primacy and the extent to which it can be adjusted. This article sits on the premise that the ordering of penalties is primarily defined and confined by the desert rationale that 'the penal sanction should fairly reflect the degree of reprehensibleness ... of the actor's

---

[1] Dr. Wei Pei. Finished her Phd research at the Erasmus university Rotterdam resulting in: P. Wei, *Criminal Procedural Agreements: In China and England and Wales*, (dissertation Rotterdam), Oisterwijk: Wolf Legal Publisher, 2015.
[2] See Dolinko 2011, pp. 403-440.
[3] For discussion about the relationship between 'just desert' and the consequentialism rationales, and the impact of such a relationship on sentencing, see, e.g.: Von Hirsch and Ashworth 2005; Pei 2015.

conduct'.[4] Consequentialist's rationales, as ulterior factors and where rewording the offender's cooperation belongs to, can be relied upon but not substantially alter that order. This premise is also consistent with the current sentencing strategies in China and England and Wales. Both legal systems have developed sentencing guidelines during the past decades, which restate in common that the overriding principle in sentencing is to match the severity of the punishment with the culpability of the accused and the harmfulness of the offence.[5]

Given such a context, this article aims to explore guidelines for maintaining proportionality between the offenders' assistance and criminal justice authorities' concessions in the operation of criminal justice, by comparing the legal regimes in China and England and Wales. Before the discussion can start several concepts need to be clarified. It should be noticed that the offender and the criminal justice authorities can cooperate in various ways, such as plea bargaining, and this research focuses only on the cooperation based on the offender's assistance against other suspects or crimes.[6] In different legal systems, similar mechanisms that contain mutually beneficial cooperation of this type are named differently, such as '*pentiti*', '*repentis*', '*kroongetuige*' and '*kronzeuge*'.[7] And the suspect or defendant who provides information or testimony is quite often referred to by derogatory names such as 'snitch',[8] 'rat',[9] or 'supergrass'.[10] To maintain clarity and objectivity, in the following discussion the suspect or defendant who provides assistance is generally referred to as a 'cooperator'.[11]

When we talk about 'assistants', 'cooperators', or 'informants' involved in criminal proceedings, these terms do not necessarily refer to an accused person. People who provide assistance can also be ordinary citizens who are either altruistic or have a legal duty, or the paid 'insiders' planted into certain criminal organizations by criminal justice authorities.[12] The cooperation studied in this research only cover

---

[4] Von Hirsch and Ashworth 2005, p. 4.
[5] For general introduction and the evolvement of the English version, see Roberts 2013a. For the Chinese version and its comparison with the English version, see Roberts and Pei 2015.
[6] It is quite often to take this type of cooperation as a part of plea bargaining. However, rewarding assisting offenders and plea bargaining are fundamentally differentiated in the rationales and aims they serve, the mechanism of their operation, and the concrete procedural rules. See Pei 2015.
[7] See Vervaele 2009, pp. 100-101.
[8] Harris 2000.
[9] Simons 2003.
[10] (1987) 9 Cr. App. R. (S.) 155.
[11] Notice that some scholars further divide cooperative offenders into two types: paid informants, and immunized informants. In this thesis only the latter will be discussed, for the former has no connection to conviction or sentence. See Limbert 2001.
[12] A brief introduction to these types of 'informants' can be seen in Grabosky 1992.

those where the assistants are themselves offenders with their own crimes being investigated, prosecuted or tried. This cooperation has two major characteristics. First, it is a state-citizen relationship established after the criminal conducts of the accused have been detected and before the litigation against him has ended. Secondly, the cooperator has two identities: a person under criminal charge, and the information provider. There is a special situation where the assistance of the offender takes the form of giving testimony in court. In such a context, the dual-identity of the cooperative offender transforms into that of the accused on the one hand, and the witness on the other hand.

Aside from the introduction (section one and conclusion (section five), the article contains three sections. In the first two sections the historical development and the current legal regimes with respect to using the offender's assistance in China and England and Wales are examined respectively. They especially pay attention to the bargaining chips offered by the two parties in such a cooperative relationship. The third section moves on to analyze two major issues in maintaining proportionality: the proper credits for cooperative offenders, and the punishment for uncooperative offenders. Based on them some guidelines for maintaining the proportionality between criminality and penalty are offered in the last section.

1. Meritorious Service (*ligong*) in China

In China the assistance offered by an accused person to criminal justice agencies against other crimes or offenders is generally termed 'meritorious service'. The current legal framework of meritorious service can be traced back to 1949 when the new government came into office. The criminal policy at that time was 'leniency to those who confess, and severity to those who resist; concession for meritorious service, and reward for major meritorious service (*tanbaicongkuan, kangjucongyan, ligongzhezui, lidagongshoujiang*)'.[13] It was initially tailored to counter-revolution activities, but later it became one of the fundamental criminal policies in China in solving all types of crimes.[14]

---

[13] See Dong Biwu, 关于肃清一切反革命分子的报告 (Report on the Elimination of the Counter-revolutionary Elements) in the Second Session of the Second National Committee of the Chinese People's Political Consultative Conference (*CPPCC*). Available at: <http://news.xinhuanet.com/ziliao/2004-10/11/content_2075766.htm> Accessed 23 September 2012.

[14] Ma Kechang 1992, p. 52.

After the Cultural Revolution (1966-1976), China re-constructed its criminal justice system by promulgating new Criminal Law (CL) and Criminal Procedure Law (CPL). The 1979 CL inherited the old practice of encouraging meritorious service, and more importantly, it translated criminal policy into concrete law provisions (Article 63). According to the 1979 CL, the criminal sanction of an offender who had committed serious crime(s) may be reduced or even exempted if he voluntarily turned himself in ***and*** meanwhile provided meritorious service.

In the following decades, the independent value of meritorious service was gradually recognized especially in crimes involving drugs and corruption. For instance, the Supplementary Regulations on Punishing Bribery and Graft (1988 Supplementary Regulations)[15] explicitly enumerated voluntary surrender, remorse and meritorious service as separate mitigation factors in sentencing. With this in mind, the 1979 CL was revised in 1997 and, since then, meritorious service has been legally recognized as an independent mitigating factor. The current legal regime with respect to meritorious service mainly consists of the 1997 CL and its eighth amendment in 2011, the 2012 CPL, and relevant judicial interpretations. The following discussion mainly focuses on two issues: the meritorious service offered by the cooperator, and the legal concessions offered by criminal justice authorities.

1.1 Cooperator's Meritorious Service

Article 68 of the 1997 CL lays the legal foundation for the cooperation. It stipulates that the accused who have performed normal meritorious service by exposing other persons' crimes, which can be verified by investigators, or who have provided important clues leading to a successful investigation of other cases, ***can*** (not shall) be given a sentence reduction or mitigation;[16] those who have performed major meritorious performance ***can*** (not shall) be given a sentence reduction or even exemption.

According to this provision, two types of meritorious service are recognized: one is to expose other's criminal conducts, and the other is to provide important clues in the investigation of other crimes. Later the Supreme People's Court (SPC)[17] added

---

[15] See关于惩治贪污贿赂罪的补充规定, *President Decree* No. 63.

[16] In Chinese CL, a 'reduction' means to reduce the sanction to a level lower than the minimum sanctions prescribed by law; while a 'mitigation' means to reduce the sanction within the sentencing scope in law.

[17] There are four levels of courts in China: basic people's courts, intermediate people's courts, higher people's courts, and the Supreme People's Court. The SPC has the power to issue

another three types through judicial interpretations (the 1998 SPC Interpretations):[18] (1) assisting criminal justice agencies in the capture of other criminal suspects (including accomplices); (2) preventing other persons' criminal activities; and (3) particular services benefiting the society.

The 1998 SPC Interpretations also adopted two criteria to distinguish normal meritorious service and major meritorious service. To be recognized as 'major meritorious service', the cooperator's assistance shall target either at suspects who may be imposed life imprisonment or death penalty, or at crimes that have significant impact on the social order.

In the cases involving criminal or mafia-like organizations, the value of meritorious service is also relevant to the culpability of the targeted offenders, and the SPC's interpretations distinguish three situations: [19] (1) a prime culprit reports to or assists investigators in arresting accomplices who are less guilty of the crime; (2) a prime culprit reports to or assists investigators in arresting accomplices who are equally culpable of the crime; and (3) an accomplice in a joint crime or a member at the bottom level of a criminal organization. The sanctions for the cooperator are differentiated accordingly. In the first situation, the court ***shall not*** issue a lenient sentence. In the second case, the court ***can*** consider mitigating the punishment. And in the third situation, the court ***shall*** impose lenient sanctions if the cooperator assists investigators in arresting prime culprits.

1.2 Legal Concessions from Criminal Justice Authorities

The cooperator's assistance is not offered for nothing. Instead, it always aims at gaining some credits in the case of his own. In the current legal regime the most common form of the credits is lenient sanction. In the SPC's Sentencing Guiding

---

judicial interpretations and other legal documents to interpret laws and to instruct courts across the country.

[18] Article 5 of 最高人民法院关于处理自首和立功具体应用法律若干问题的解释 (the SPC Interpretations on Several Legal Issues on the Application of Voluntary Surrender and Meritorious Performance), 法释[1998] 8号 (*Fashi*[1998] No. 8), issued and validated on 9 May 1998, available at: <http://www.law-lib.com/law/law_view.asp?id=13925>. Accessed 15 May 2014.

[19] 高人民法院处理自首和立功若干具体问题的意见 (Opinions on Several Specific Issues on Voluntary Surrender and Meritorious Service in 2010), 法发[2010] 60号 (*Fafa* [2010] No. 60), issued and validated on 22 December 2010, available at: <http://vip.chinalawinfo.com/newlaw2002/slc/slc.asp?db=chl&gid=143184>. Accessed 15 May 2014.

Opinions on Common Crimes (2014 Guiding Opinions),[20] a graduated sentencing discount system for meritorious service is established in accordance with the value of the assistance. The maximum discounts for meritorious service range between 20% and 50%; in exceptional cases the punishment can be exempted.[21] The 2014 Guiding Opinions are applicable only in crimes where the maximum sentence is lower than life imprisonment. As to more serious crimes, Article 251 of the 2012 CPL stipulates that the death penalty shall not be executed if the offender exposed any major crimes of other persons, or provided other major meritorious service.

A subsequent question is whether the cooperative offender can obtain other types of concession apart from sentencing discount, especially immunity of prosecution. In China the public prosecution services follow the principle of legality instead of expediency, and therefore their power in ceasing prosecution is quite limited. According to the 2012 CPL, prosecutors cannot abstain from prosecution unless two conditions are satisfied simultaneously: (1) the charged crime is minor, and (2) the criminal punishment is unnecessary or can be exempted according to the 1997 CL.[22] The former condition normally refers to crimes carrying a maximum sentence lower than three years' imprisonment. The key question lies on the second condition as to whether assistance could render the offender exempt from punishment, or make the punishment unnecessary. In the 1997 CL, cooperators who provided major meritorious service and had voluntarily turned himself in ***should*** be exempted from punishment (Article 68 of the 1997 CL). However, the eighth amendment of the 1997 CL in 2011abolished this rule, indicating that the cooperator may still serve penalties even if both voluntary surrender and major meritorious service are fulfilled.

---

[20] 关于常见犯罪的量刑指导意见，法发[2013] 14号(*Fafa* [2013] No. 14), issued on 23 December 2013 and validated on 1 January 2014. Available at: <http://en.pkulaw.cn/display.aspx?cgid=221534&lib=law>. Accessed on 18 August 2014. The Chinese research on sentencing guidelines started from 2008 when the SPC promoted the unification of sentencing in 12 local people's courts (basic and intermediate levels). In 2010 this experiment was expanded to people's courts on basic and intermediate levels across the country. Three years later, the SPC revised the guidelines and required all peoples' courts to stipulate detailed regulations and implement them before the end of 2014. The guidelines aim at enhancing the quality of sentencing on one hand, and promoting consistency in adjudication on the other hand.

[21] Section 5 of the 2014 Guiding Opinions.

[22] Article 173 of the 2012 CPL.

2. Rewarding Assisting Offenders in England and Wales

As to England and Wales, Lord Bingham stated in *R v A and B*[23] that 'it has been the long-standing practice of the courts to recognize by a further discount... the help given, and expected to be given, to the authorities in the investigation, detection, suppression and prosecution of serious crime'. The systematic use of cooperators in the modernized criminal justice system in England and Wales can be traced back to the early 1970s as a direct consequence of the increase in serious organized crimes, especially bank robberies, in and around London.[24] For instance, in the *Bertie Smalls* case, the offender entered into a written agreement with the Director of Public Prosecutions (DPP), Sir Norman Skelhom, and obtained total immunity by giving 'Queen's evidence' – evidence or testimony given by an accused or convicted criminal to the state against his accomplices – against dozens of his co-offenders in the charges of bank robberies and other criminal activities.[25] Small's case showed a path for other career criminals at that time, and many of them, such as Maurice O'Mahoney[26] and Charlie Lowe,[27] offered evidence against hundreds of their co-offenders to gain themselves sentencing reductions.

In the 1980s, the popularity of such practices declined because serious problems emerged about the use of cooperators, including 'police corruption, the use of particularly unfavorable supergrasses and major failures in witness protection arrangements'.[28] However, in the 1990s the practice of encouraging cooperation rose again. The new policy paper 'Tackling Crime Effectively' at that time expressed a strong recommendation for new policing techniques against a backdrop of 'ever rising crime rates and decreasing clear-up rates', and declared informants as 'the lifeblood of CID (Criminal Investigation Department)'.[29] In 2004 the Home Office issued the White Paper *One Step Ahead*, proposing to enshrine the long-standing practice into statute so that assistance from offenders could be obtained and used

---

[23] *R v A and B* [1999] 1 Cr. App. R. (S.) 52.
[24] Greer 1995, p. 520.
[25] Morton 2006.
[26] About the story of the famous supergrass Maurice O'Mahnoney, one can refer to his autobiography: O'Mahoney and Wooding 1978.
[27] *Lowe*, (1978) 66 Cr. App. R. 122.
[28] Martin 2013, p. 274. Later in this section the author will go into further detail about the mal-practice during these periods which originated from the application of assistance agreement.
[29] Audit Commission, *Helping with Enquiries: Tackling Crime Effectively* (Police Paper No. 12) (London: HMSO, 1993).

more effectively, especially in dealing with organized crimes and serious crimes.[30] It led to the promulgation of the Serious Organized Crime and Police Act in 2005 (SOCPA 2005), in which the use of assisting cooperators gained statutory basis.

2.1 Cooperator's Assistance

For a long time there have been discussions about what kind of assistance offered by the cooperator could be rewarded, and controversies once mainly focused on whether such assistance bore any relation to the crimes committed by the cooperator himself. At first judges were reluctant to grant credit for 'supergrasses' – cooperators who turn into witnesses in the court trial of crimes irrelevant to their own. For instance, in *R v Preston* in 1987, the Court held that 'what the courts should not take into account … is evidence of information given by any accused person who does not relate to the crime of which he stands charged'.[31]

Such an attitude, however, has gradually changed in a series of cases such as *R v Sivan* in 1988. In this case the Court of Appeal extended the scope of an assistance by restating that 'the judge should tailor the sentence so as to punish the defendant but at the same time reward him so far as possible for the help he had given in order to demonstrate to others that it was worth their while to disclose the criminal activities of others for the benefit of the law-abiding public in general'.[32]

As to the value of the assistance, the general principle established in case law is that it is based on 'the value to the administration of justice of his performance of the agreement, not on the simple fact that the agreement had been performed'.[33]Accordingly, three key factors have been recognized in the English legal system: (1) 'the degree of assistance provided'; (2) 'the nature and effect of the information imparted'; and (3) 'the degree of risk to which the defendant by his actions exposed himself and his family'.[34]

The first factor mainly concerns whether the assistance is in the form of pre-trial intelligence, or 'Queen's evidence' during court trial. The latter is normally

---

[30] Home Office, *One Step Ahead: A 21st Century Strategy to Defeat Organised Crime*, available at: <http://www.archive2.official-documents.co.uk/document/cm61/6167/6167.pdf>. Accessed 24 October 2013.

[31] *R. v Preston* (1987) 9 Cr. App. R. (S.) 155.

[32] (1988) 87 Cr. App. R. 407.

[33] *R. v D*, [2011] 1 Cr. App. R. (S.) 69.

[34] *Sivan*, (1988) 87 Cr. App. R. 407.

considered to be of enhanced value.[35] For the second factor, the general rule is that the value of the assistance can be enhanced if it 'produces convictions for the most serious offences ... or prevents them, or which leads to the disruption of or indeed the breakup of major criminal gangs'.[36] As to the factor of risk, it is usually considered as the 'greatest disincentive to the provision of assistance to the authorities', and 'the greater the nature of the criminality, the greater the consequent risk'.[37] One approach adopted by the legislator in order to balance that disincentive, is to raise the counterparties' offer: the higher the risk, the larger the discount.[38] In *R v A*, for instance, a sentence reduction from 13 years' imprisonment to five years was upheld by the Court of Appeal on the basis of a 'real and might be continuing' risk for the defendant and his family because of giving evidence.[39]

2.2 Legal Concessions from Criminal Justice Authorities

The forms of legal concessions offered by the criminal justice authorities correspond with the stage at which they are issued. At the pre-trial stage, under the SOCPA 2005 the concession can take two forms. The first one is prosecution immunity (s71) where a specified prosecutor can issue a written immunity notice to a suspect for the purposes of investigation or prosecution of other crimes. Prosecution immunity can only be applied in exceptional situations, i.e., when the assistance is related to an offence capable of being tried in the Crown Court (s113 of CJA 2009). The second form is the 'restricted use undertakings' (s72), which 'enables the prosecutor to offer an undertaking not to use certain evidence in criminal proceedings or civil confiscation proceedings'.[40] The purpose of such arrangement is to avoid the conflict between cooperation and the right against self-incrimination. However, it cannot exempt the accused person completely from prosecution. It also does not prevent the use of 'other evidence' that may lead to successful conviction of the cooperator.

In 2013 the Crime and Courts Act (CCA 2013) introduced 'deferred prosecution agreement' (DPA) into the English criminal justice system. A DPA refers to 'an agreement reached under juridical supervision ... allows a prosecution to be

---

[35] *R. v D*, [2011] 1 Cr. App. R. (S.) 69.

[36] *R.v P; R v Blackburn*, [2007] EWCA Crim 2290; *R. v A and B*, [1999] 1 Cr. App. R. (S.) 52.

[37] *R.v P; and R. v Blackburn*, [2007] EWCA Crim 2290.

[38] Andrew et al 2010, p. 442.

[39] Thomas 2006.

[40] Goldsmith 2006, p. 29.

suspended for a defined period provided [a commercial] organization meets certain specified conditions'.[41] Failing to do so, the organization will be prosecuted and can be held criminally responsible. According to s17 of CCA 2013, one of the conditions for DPA is that the accused organization should 'co-operate in any investigation related to the alleged offence'. Under this scheme, deferring prosecution becomes part of the prosecutorial toolkit for making use of cooperators.

Once the cooperator's case enters into the court trial, the most common form of concession is sentencing reduction based on the evidence of cooperation provided by the public prosecutor. The sentencing guidelines issued by the Sentencing Council do not specify the credits or percentage for the discount. The general rule is that the judge should 'tailor the sentence so as to punish the defendant but at the same time reward him so far as possible for [his] help'.[42] Even so, some rules have been developed in case law. Normally the reduction for the defendant's assistance is between one half and two thirds, and only in the most exceptional cases can the reduction exceed three quarters.[43]

3. Balancing Cooperation and Concession to Maintain Proportionality in Sentencing

In his research on the use of cooperators in criminal justice, Stephen Schulhofer noticed a 'cooperation paradox' that 'defendants who are most in the know, and thus have the most "substantial assistance" to offer, are often those who are most centrally involved in conspiratorial crimes'.[44] Such a paradox is confirmed by the legal regimes in the two jurisdictions, namely that the most important factor in evaluating the assistance and issuing corresponding legal concessions is its actual effect in solving other crimes. As stated in *One Step Ahead*, using assisting offenders has at least four merits: (1) speed up trials; (2) enhance prosecutions'

---

[41] SFO, *Deferred Prosecution Agreements: New Guidance for Prosecutors*, issued on the 14th of February 2014, available at: <http://www.sfo.gov.uk/press-room/latest-press-releases/press-releases-2013/deferred-prosecution-agreements-new-guidance-for-prosecutors.aspx>. Accessed 15th of April 2014.

[42] *Sivan*, (1988) 87 Cr. App. R. 407.

[43] *R v P; and R. v Blackburn*, [2007] EWCA Crim 2290.

[44] In his research Stephen Schulhofer considers 'cooperation paradox' as the one of the major factors which impairs the validity of legal provisions. See Schulhofer 1993, p. 212.

impact; (3) approach major criminals; and (4) erode trust within criminal gangs.[45] What is reflected in these merits is a utilitarian rationale, and, derived from it, a tendency to depart from the retributivist's proportionality between the severity of a sanction and the degree of criminality. How to maintain equilibrium between concession and cooperation is a tough question confronted by the legislator, prosecutors and judges in China and England and Wales. To answer this question, two issues need to be examined: the appropriate credits, and the punishment for uncooperative offenders.

3.1 Appropriate Credits for Assistance

Whether or not the credit for the cooperation is appropriate depends on answers to three questions. The first question concerns factors that should be considered by criminal justice authorities in assigning credits. The analysis above shows that, apart from the nature and effect of the assistance, which are in common in the two legal systems, the English legal rules also pay attention to two other factors: the form of the assistance, and the risk to the cooperative offender. These two factors are actually co-related, as exposing oneself in a public trial as a Crown witness may significantly increase the risk of the cooperator being avenged, especially when there involves a criminal gang.[46] The general rules here are, as aforementioned, higher rewards are given for providing Queen's evidence, and the higher the risk, the higher the concession. In China, however, neither factor affects the legal concessions. It is mainly because on the one hand, the inquisitorial tradition relies heavily on the dossier prepared at the pre-trial stage, while on the other hand, giving testimony in court is not obligatory for most of the witnesses.

Since the 1990s these two factors have changed as the Chinese criminal justice system is gradually transforming from 'a traditional inquisitorial system of justice into a more adversarial legal process'.[47] In the 1979 CPL and the 1996 CPL only the written statement of the witness needed to be examined in court, and no penalties would follow if the witness refused his attendance.[48] Although the 2012 CPL still generally recognizes the validity of the witness' statement (Article 59), the attendance of the witness becomes compulsory if (1) parties have disputes about the

---

[45] Home Office, *One Step Ahead: A 21st Century Strategy to Defeat Organised Crime*, available at: <http://www.archive2.official-documents.co.uk/document/cm61/6167/6167.pdf>. Accessed 31 October 2013.

[46] Elliott 1999.

[47] Hong and Miethe 2003, p. 554.

[48] Article 36 of the 1979 CPL and Article 47 of the 1996 CPL.

statement; (2) the statement may significantly influence conviction and sentencing; ***and*** (3) the court considers it as necessary (Article 187). With such a trend, the emphasis of criminal proceedings would gradually shift from the pre-trial to the trial stage, enhancing the value of the oral testimony, and meanwhile increasing the risk of exposing the identity of the cooperator. In this sense, it would be more appropriate to take the form of the assistance and the risk of the cooperator into consideration.

The second question is in what form the credits can be assigned to the cooperation. As mentioned earlier, cooperative offenders in England and Wales may receive four types of rewards: restricted undertakings, prosecution immunity, deferred prosecution, and sentence discount. The first three options are less used because restricted undertakings will not terminate the litigation, a prosecution immunity notice can only be exceptionally applied, and only certain organizations qualify for DPA. In China, 'restricted use undertakings' and 'deferred prosecution' do not exist in the current criminal proceedings, and non-prosecution decisions can hardly be issued in the case of meritorious service due to the principle of legality.

Therefore the common approach adopted in both legal systems in rewarding the cooperation is sentencing discount, but still a major distinction can be observed: in England and Wales the offender's assistance is simply listed as a mitigating factor in the definitive guidelines, while in China the 2014 Guiding Opinions provide clear numerical guidance regarding the degree to which specific factors should affect the sentence. This distinction is to a large extent due to the function of the sentencing guidelines. Although both the definitive guidelines in England and Wales and the 2014 Guiding Opinions in China serve some common objectives such as equality and consistency in sentencing, the Chinese guidelines also bear the function of assisting individual judges and local courts to resist extra-judicial interference. For instance, when confronted with adverse public reaction to a specific sentence, the court can point to the numerical guidelines to support its decision.[49]

The most exceptional prize for a cooperator is exemption of punishment. From previous discussion it can be observed that both legal systems maintain the possibility of full exemption, and an crucial question here is under what circumstances such reward can be granted. In England and Wales, immunity from prosecution and DPA are two approaches to enable the avoidance of further litigation, and, though under the judicial supervision, it is the public prosecutor in charge. Judges may also exempt the cooperator, not based on numerical instructions but judges' discretion. In comparison, in the Chinese criminal justice system exemption can hardly be issued during prosecution, while judges can make such a

[49] This is similar to what Björn Ahl once noticed in the guiding cases system in China. See Ahl 2014.

decision when, as stipulated in the 2014 Guiding Opinions, the cooperator offers major meritorious service and meanwhile he is charged with an extremely minor crime.

Notwithstanding the possibility of exemption, both legal systems have acknowledged the general principle that it should only be used in exceptional situations. For instance, in the Smalls' case mentioned earlier, with awareness of the cooperator's strategy, the agreement in that case was ruled as an 'unholy deal', and the law lords demanded that future supergrasses should not be completely exempted from imprisonment.[50] As to China, the revisions in the eighth amendment of the 1997 CL with respect to the exemption of cooperative offenders also reflect the prudent attitude of the legislator towards such a decision.

3.2 Sanctions on Non-Cooperation

The proportionate sentence of the cooperator can be violated not only by undue mitigation, as discussed in the former section, but also by improper sanctions on non-cooperation. The latter focuses on the question of how to prevent the mutually beneficial 'concession for cooperation' exchange, a comparatively fair deal, from being downgraded into 'punishment for non-cooperation', a pure use of coercion. It derives from the premise that assisting criminal justice authorities in investigation, prosecution and conviction is normally not a legal obligation of the accused. Unless amounting to contempt of court refusing cooperation should lead to the ordinary disposals rather than, for instance, enhanced sentence. In the case of giving testimony in court, the cooperator bears the obligations and privileges as normal witnesses. For his own crime, based on which the cooperation deal was offered by criminal justice authorities, there still should not be any aggravation in sanctions due to non-cooperation. In other words, there should be a mid-ground between 'mitigation' and 'aggrevation'.

At the prosecution stage this issue is less problematic. It is because the available options are relatively clear: prosecution, non-prosecution, or, as in DPA, deferred prosecution. The basic rule is also relatively simple: non-cooperation will initiate prosecution, which can hardly be deemed as a 'sanction'. It should be noticed here that although the Chinese public prosecutors are restricted in issuing non-

---

[50] Cahal Milmo, 'Bertie Smalls: Quiet Death of the Original Supergrass', *The Independent*, 7th of February 2014, available at: <http://www.independent.co.uk/news/uk/crime/bertie-smalls-quiet-death-of-the-original-supergrass-781020.html>. Accessed 7th of February 2014.

prosecution decisions, they can, unlike their English colleagues, make sentencing proposals to judges. Although such proposals are not legally binding, they will inevitably influence judges' assessment on the cooperation as well as their decision on concessions.[51]

In contrast, whether the cooperator receives proper credits after he has fully performed the contractual obligation is less obvious in judges' decisions. It is because the sentencing range for a certain criminal act is normally a continuous spectrum with grey areas. For instance, in China the sentence for normal robbery ranges from three to seven years' imprisonment. Within this range the judge can choose any period of custody based on his discretion. In fact, the aforementioned slogan 'leniency to those who confess, and severity to those who resist' in China shows typically an absence of such a mid-ground.

3.3 Visibility of Mitigation, Aggravation, and Mid-Ground

Whether the law assigns proper credits and withholds undue punishment is one question, whereas whether 'carrots and sticks' can be detected in reality is quite another. In fact, the later question defines the actual and material impact of the cooperation on legal decisions especially in sentencing. As both legal systems have promulgated sentencing guidelines, this question can be further rephrased as whether or not judges comply with the guidelines in considering the cooperation. One way to observe judges' compliance is to examine the final verdicts. For example, the first instance judgment of *R v Kiely*[52] in 2009 clearly stated that '... a further 30 per cent reduction would be allowed to reflect ... assistance which the appellant had given the prosecution in relation to other matters'. After the second instance trial the Court of Appeal further confirmed that '[w]e agree that overall insufficient discount was given for the assistance that was given'.

In China, however, the situation is different. On the one hand, the 2014 Guiding Opinions list detailed sentencing discount for different types of meritorious service, while on the other hand, the final judgments normally do not reflect the actual reduction but only mention mitigating and aggravating factors together. For instance, in Zhou XX's case of trading drugs in 2005, the verdict of the first instance trial only stated that 'the court is satisfied that the defendant was a first time offender, that he committed meritorious service, and that he confessed. Therefore,

[51] See Chen 2011.
[52] *R v Kiely*, [2009] EWCA Crim 756.

lenient punishment can be imposed'.[53] Without clarifying the starting point of the sentence and the extent of the discount in the verdicts, judges' compliance with the guidelines can hardly be monitored or evaluated.

Apart from the verdicts, the compliance with sentencing guidelines and the prevention of undue aggravation in sanctions require systematic statistical analysis. In England and Wales, the Criminal Justice Act 2009 requires the English Council to monitor the operation and effectiveness of the definitive guidelines. As a result of this duty, the Crown Court Sentencing Survey (CCSS) was launched in England and Wales to determine the level of judicial compliance with the guidelines.[54] To date, neither the SPC nor the local judiciary in China has introduced a court-based survey of this kind. Therefore, no data are available to evaluate the compliance rate or the effect of the 2014 Guidelines on judicial practice.

4. Conclusions

After the comparative analysis, one can at least draw two conclusions. First, it is not rare for criminal justice agencies to encourage an accused person to assisting investigation, prosecution and conviction, by offering him certain types of concession. In fact, both legal systems have shown a similar trend that such a practice is likely to be strengthened especially in the areas where the normal approaches appear to be less effective in solving crimes. Second, with this trend the two legal systems are confronted with the tough task of balancing cooperation and legal concessions so that the proportionality between the criminality of the offender and the criminal sanctions can be preserved. It requires not only proper credits to be assigned to different types of assistance, but also necessary safeguards against undue punishment on those who refuse to cooperate.

Arising from these two observations are three propositions. First, in deciding proper sanctions for the accused person, the basic principle is that the seriousness of the crime should be the major and primary factor in deciding penal sanctions. Therefore the full exemption of penalty should be used only in exceptional situations. Second, in evaluating the cooperation, not only its detection value but also the form of the assistance and the risk to the cooperator should be taken into consideration. Third, new approaches should be developed to make the sentencing process more visible to mitigate the risk of punishing uncooperative offenders inappropriately.

---

[53] (2005)中一法刑一初字(*ZhongyifaxingyiChuzi*) No. 65.

[54] For general introduction and the latest findings of the survey, see Julian Roberts 2013b.

Through examining the legal regimes in China and England and Wales, two approaches can be helpful in this respect. On the one hand, the legal decisions should contain the following elements: the original decision based on the criminality of the accused and the harmfulness of the crime, the value of the cooperation, the corresponding credits, the final disposals, and reasons for any deviation from the normal credit. On the other hand, in legal systems where guidelines have been issued with respect to rewarding the cooperator, statistics on the compliance of criminal justice authorities should be collected, assessed, and monitored systematically.

Bibliography

Ahl 2014

B. Ahl, 'Retaining Judicial Professionalism: The New Guiding Cases Mechanism of the Supreme People's Court', 217 (2014) *China Quarterly*, 121-139.

Andrew et al. 2010

S. Andrew et al., *Criminal Justice,* Oxford: Oxford University Press, 2010.

Chen 2011

R. Chen, '论量刑建议' (On Sentencing Proposals), 2(2011) 政法论坛 (*Tribune of Political Science and Law*), 14-28.

Dolinko 2011

D. Dolinko, 'Punishment', in John Deign and David Dolinko (eds.), *The Oxford Handbook of Philosophy of Criminal Law*, New York: Oxford University Press, 2011.

Elliott 1999

D.W. Elliott, 'Securing the Evidence of Criminal Associates', May (1999) *Criminal Law Review*, 349-362.

Goldsmith 2006

The Lord Goldsmith QC, 'The New Powers to Tackle Organized Crime and the Role of the Prosecutor', (2006) *Inter Alia*, 5: 28-31.

Grabosky 1992

P.N. Grabosky, 'Prosecutors, Informants, and the Integrity of the Criminal Justice System', 4 (1992) *Current Issues Crim. Just.,* 47-63.

Greer 1995

S. Greer, 'Towards a Sociological Model of the Police Informant', 46(3) (1995) *The British Journal of Sociology*, 509-527.

Harris 2000

G.C. Harris, 'Testimony for Sale: The Law and Ethics of Snitches and Experts', 28 (2000) *Pepp. L. Rev.,* 1-74.

Von Hirsch & Ashworth 2005

A. von Hirsch & A. Ashworth, *Proportionate Sentencing*, Oxford: Oxford University Press, 2005.

Hong & Miethe 2003

L. Hong & T.D. Miethe, 'Confessions and Criminal Case Disposition in China', 37(3) (2003) *Law and Society Review*, 549-578.

Kechang 1999

M. Kechang, 刑事政策学 (*On Criminal Policy*), Wuhan: Wuhan University Press, 1999.

Limbert 2001

M. Limbert, 'Problems Associated with Prosecutorial Control over Filing Substantial Assistance Motions and a Proposal for Substantial Assistance Pre-sentence Hearing', 27 (2001) *J. Legis.,* 251-268.

Martin 2013

R.Martin, 'The Recent Supergrass Controversy: Have We Learnt from the Troubled Past?', 4 (2013) *Criminal Law Review*, 273-289.

Morton 2006

J. Morton, 'Helping Prosecutors with Their Inquiries', 70(3) (2006) *Journal of Criminal Law*, 183-185.

O'Mahoney & Wooding 1978

M. O'Mahoney & D. Wooding, *King Squealer: True Story of Maurice O'Mahoney*, London: W. H. Allen, 1978.

Pei 2015

W. Pei, *Criminal Procedural Agreements: In China and England and Wales*, (dissertation Rotterdam), Oisterwijk: Wolf Legal Publisher, 2015.

Roberts 2013a

J.V. Roberts, 'Sentencing Guidelines in England and Wales: Recent Developments and Emerging Issues', 76(1)(2013) *Law and Contemporary Problems*, 1-25.

Roberts 2013b

J.V. Roberts 'Sentencing Guidelines: New Findings from the Crown Court Survey', in Andrew Ashworth and Julia V. Roberts (eds.), Sentencing guidelines, Oxford: Oxford University press, 2013.

Roberts & Pei 2015

J.V. Roberts & W. Pei, 'Structuring Judicial Discretion in China: Exploring the 2014 Sentencing Guidelines', (2015) *Criminal Law Forum*, 1-31.

Schulhofer 1993

S.J. Schulhofer, 'Rethinking Mandatory Minimums', 28 (1993) *Wake Forest Law Review*, 199-222.

Simons 2003

M.A. Simons, 'Retribution for Rats: Cooperation, Punishment, and Atonement', 56(1) (2003) *Vanderbilt Law Review,* 1-54.

Thomas 2006

D.A. Thomas, 'Sentencing: Assistance Given by Offender – Assistance Given after Conviction and Sentence', Dec. (2006) *Criminal Law Review,* 1079-1082.

Vervaele 2009

J.A.E. Vervaele, 'Special Procedural Measures and the Protection of Human Rights, General Report', 5(2) (2009) *Utrecht Law Review*, 66-103.

Expert evidence in criminal legal proceedings: three approaches to ensuring the accuracy of expert evidence in criminal proceedings

Mark Visser[1]

Introduction

'Current legal approaches to complex criminality' was the subject of the PhD Day 2014. The question that immediately comes to mind is what makes criminality complex? To this question there are several possible answers. To commit certain offences may be complex because it requires the offenders to have specialist (technical) knowledge. An example of such an offence is hacking into a government database.[2] Complexity can also derive from the number and concurrence of (international) laws that apply to an offence. Examples of such offences are cross-border drug trafficking, human trafficking and money laundering.[3] The complex character of criminality can also simply derive from the fact that the judiciary lacks the knowledge needed to assess the underlying facts of a case. In theory this phenomenon can occur in any given case relating to any given offence. For instance a simple case of embezzlement can suddenly become complex when the offenders made use of specialist tools or knowledge in committing the offence. A case of abuse can become complex when questions arise concerning the mental health of the supposed offender. It is that hiatus in the knowledge of the judiciary that calls for the involvement of experts.

---

[1] Mr. M. (Mark) Visser, PhD candidate at the Open Universiteit.

[2] The Dutch military is supposedly under attack from hackers on a daily basis. See: <http://www.nu.nl/internet/4230954/defensie-slaat-dagelijks-cyberaanvallen-van-andere-landen-af.html>.

[3] The suspicions of money laundering surrounding bitcoin provide an example: <www.reuters.com/article/2014/03/24/us-bitcoin-europol-money-laundering-idUSBREA2N1A420140324>.

The growing need for expert advice in criminal proceedings[4] is just another example of the increasingly complex nature of criminality in general.[5] Effective investigations and prosecution of criminality is becoming more and more dependent on experts.[6] The involvement of experts from different fields of expertise in legal proceedings also entails risks. It is ultimately up to the judge to decide whether or not to use the expert advice. However, the judge who is exclusively competent to answer the question regarding the guilt of a defendant may in fact have little choice other than to rely on the information provided to him by the expert because it may well prove to be indispensable in interpreting the facts of the case. The paradox is how to ascertain that the information provided by the expert is indeed correct and, moreover, relevant to the legal question at hand.[7] In a lot of cases the judge will lack the knowledge needed to verify every aspect of the information provided by the expert. It is in fact this knowledge gap[8] that explains the need for an expert advice.

1. Three approaches

In general there are three possible approaches to deal with the aforementioned paradox and to ensure, as much as possible, that the information provided by the experts is accurate.

The first approach is to ensure that the experts meet a minimum set of criteria that establish them as an expert in their field. In the Netherlands these criteria are codified.[9] The aim is to ensure, up front, that the information, provided by experts that meet the required criteria is of a certain, high, quality.

---

[4] J. de Ridder *et al* 2014, p. 69; Jaarrapport NFI 2015, p.5, available at: <www.forensischinstituut.nl/kenniscentrum/publicaties/jaarverslagen/index.aspx?action=0>.

[5] About the growing need for (complex) expert advice in relatively simple criminal cases see: Crijns, Van der Meij en Ten Voorde 2010, p. 532; An example of a more or less accidentally complex case can be found in: De Lange 2012, p. 95.

[6] De Ridder *et al.* 2014, p. 70;Van Kempen 2012, p. 101.

[7] The starting point is that it is exclusively up to the judge to assess the evidence: Nijboer 2011, p. 70; Similar: Buruma 2009; Den Hartog 2005, p. 217; This starting point can also be found in case law of the ECHR: ECHR 15th of June 2010, 34334/04, (Ashot Harutyunyan/ Armenia), r.o. 149.

[8] Known in Dutch literature as the 'kennisparadox'. See: Dubelaar & Nijboer 2008; Crijns, Van der Meij & Ten Voorde 2010, p. 528-537; De Groot & Akkermans, p. 501; 29 % of the respondents to a 2008 survey in Vrij Nederland (among 652 employees of the judiciary of which 489 were judges) thought judges lacked the knowledge to assess expert evidence, 39 % did not answer the question: www.vn.nl/extra/pdf/enqueterechters.PDF, p. 30.

[9] Wet deskundige in strafzaken, *Staatblad* 2009, 351; Besluit register deskundige in strafzaken, *Staatblad* 2009, 330.

The second approach is to increase the availability of specialized knowledge within the judiciary. This can, for instance, be achieved by educating judges or employing specialists within the judiciary.[10]

The third and last approach is to consult more experts on the same matter. If they agree amongst each other, this increases the validity of the information.[11] If, however, the expert opinions are contradictory this should highlight to the judge specific points that need further scrutiny.[12]

This contribution will examine these three approaches to regulate the use of expert evidence in criminal proceedings.[13] It will address some bottlenecks that are inherent to the use of expert evidence and the extent to which these bottlenecks are mitigated by the three approaches. It examines the manner in which the three approaches coincide and whether they may complement each other. It will conclude by answering the question which of the three approaches, or combination thereof, is best suited to be used in present-day criminal legal proceedings.

2. Criterion

Defining a criterion suitable for answering the question central to this contribution proved to be difficult. The accuracy of expert evidence is influenced by many factors. Among these factors are ethical traits like impartiality and independence as well as factors pertaining to the capabilities of the expert like education, knowledge and experience.[14] There are also external factors such as the availability of reliable research material and the cooperation and contributions of parties. Apart from these factors there is the problem of the knowledge gap which, as mentioned earlier, often prevents the judge from verifying the information provided by the expert. Even if a suitable criterion can be defined the complexity of the underlying facts that the expert is asked to provide information on will render such a criterion difficult to use. After all, how do you assess information that you do not (fully) understand?

I will take a closer look at two possible criteria for answering the question central to this contribution.

---

[10] Specialization within the judiciary is a consideration of the government: *Kamerstukken II* 2011/12, 29 279, nr. 148.

[11] Which can be adduced in the form of a written expert report or a verbal statement.

[12] More detailed about this: M.D. Rijnsburger & M. Malsch 2013.

[13] Although the scope of this article is limited to criminal proceedings, the findings of this article also apply to other fields of law.

[14] These factors were already mentioned back in 1956 by Abma: Abma 1956, p. 10-12.

The first possible criterion that may be used is article 6 ECHR. Because article 6 ECHR contains minimum standards for legal proceedings it is a suitable starting point for examining the three approaches. In this article I am, however, searching for an optimal solution rather than one that merely complies with minimum standards.

This brings me to the second possible criterion which is truthfinding.[15] The importance of truthfinding in criminal proceedings is undisputed in Dutch legal literature,[16] case law[17] and politics.[18] Equally undisputed is the notion that 'the truth' cannot be ascertained with certainty.[19] All this begs the question as to the meaning of the word truth.[20] The Dutch dictionary defines it as:

> '*accordance with the facts / something that is true.*'[21]

Given the fact that the (appointed) expert is assisting the courts in their search for the truth,[22] it is safe to say that in order to be of any use the expert advice must be in accordance with the facts. One problem with that is that, as stated earlier, the so-called knowledge gap will effectively prevent the judge from assessing the accuracy of these facts. A second problem derives from the different meanings the term truth may (or may not) have in legal proceedings and science.[23] The scope of this article does not allow for a detailed account of such differences. One of the main differences, however, appears to be the fact that from a legal perspective truthfinding is limited by factors such as legislation and protection of party interests,[24] whereas in the empirical sciences such is not the case. It is clear that truthfinding is an important and relevant factor relating to the accuracy of expert

---

[15] This element overlaps with the first as it is an integral part of the right to a fair trial as required by art 6 ECHR: De Groot 2012, p. 68.
[16] Ten Voorde 2008, p. 1-14; Cleiren 2001, p. 16.
[17] For instance see: Hoge Raad (Supreme Court) 10th of December 2013, ECLI:NL:HR:2013:1740, *Rechtspraak van de Week* 2014, 46; Hoge Raad (Supreme Court) 30th of October 2007, ECLI:NL:HR:2007:BA5667, *Rechtspraak van de Week* 2007, 952.
[18] *Kamerstukken II* 2005/06, 30 300 VI, nr. 32, p. 1.
[19] Crijns 2008, p. 19; Nijboer 1993, p. 15; De Vries 2002, p. 16-25.
[20] In criminal (and other) proceedings truthfinding refers to the search for the material truth (materiële waarheidsvinding). More details on this term can for instance be found in: Crijns, Van der Meij & Ten Voorde 2008; De Bock 2011, p. 73-80.
[21] English translation of the definition of the word 'waarheid' in the Dutch dictionary. For the original Dutch definition see: <www.vandale.nl/opzoeken?pattern=waarheid&lang=nn#.Ux8Fevl5Mg0>.
[22] Crijns, Van der Meij & Ten Voorde 2010, p. 531-532; Equally for civil proceedings, see: De Bock 2011, p. 289.
[23] More detailed on this matter: Kwakman 2014; Mackor 2010, p. 52-66; Cleiren 2008.
[24] Similar: Kwakman 2014, p. 413.

evidence. However, the diffuse meaning(s) of the terms truth and truthfinding make these unsuitable as a strict criterion. Nevertheless, contrary to using article 6 ECHR as a criterion which only sets a minimum standard for legal proceedings, the criterion of truthfinding refers to an ideal situation and therefore seems more fitting as a criterion in light of the purpose of this contribution.

As explained, the above mentioned criteria are both unsuitable as strict criteria. They can however, be used as reference points to discuss the three approaches and their respective advantages and disadvantages. Article 6 ECHR serves as a criterion to define the minimum standards that expert reports have to meet. Contrary to that, the criterion of truthfinding sets an optimal standard that will be impossible to meet in practice. It is therefore realistic to assume that the answer to the question asked in this contribution will provide a solution situated somewhere between these two 'opposite' standards.

3. The first approach: minimum criteria

An important manner in which the quality of expert reports can be ensured is by safeguarding the quality of the experts in person. This is sought to achieve by way of requiring experts to be registered. As mentioned earlier, Dutch criminal law provides a basis for the registration of experts. The legal basis for the register itself lies in article 51k sub 1 of the Dutch code of criminal procedure (hereafter: CCP). The qualifications that the expert must meet in order to be included in the register are based upon article 51i sub 4 CCP and are specified in secondary legislation, specifically the 'Order register experts in criminal procedures' (hereafter: the Order).[25] Before having a closer look at the advantages and disadvantages of using a single register as a basis for choosing experts I would like to point out that a judge in any stage of the proceedings is not obliged to use a registered expert. Article 51k sub 2 CCP provides a basis for the use of experts who are not registered. If the judge chooses to appoint an unregistered expert he has to give reasons for this.[26]

Article 6 ECHR does not require an expert to meet certain requirements. It is left to the member States to define the term expert.[27] It is up to the judge to assess the

[25] In Dutch: Besluit register deskundige in strafzaken (*Staatblad* 2009, 330).
[26] Middelbos & Smithuis 2008.
[27] ECHR 6th of May 1985, 8658/79, *Nederlandse Jurisprudentie* 1989, 385, with annotation P. van Dijk, (Bönisch/Austria), r.o. 31.

relevance of (expert) evidence[28] and to decide whether or not to hear an expert.[29] Article 6 ECHR requires a court to give reasons for its judgment in both criminal and non-criminal proceedings.[30] This general requirement does not mean that a judge has to respond to every argument or complaint,[31] including complaints about the alleged lack of expertise on behalf of an expert.

The aim of this paragraph is not to assess every aspect of the quality of the Dutch registration practice, but rather to examine the general usefulness of such a register. Choosing the right expert is not an easy task. Anyone can call himself an expert, because the term expert is not (legally) defined. A subsequent problem is that, partly due to the knowledge gap, judges are often incapable of assessing; a) the existing fields of expertise and b) to oversee all the experts active in a particular field.[32] One advantage of a register is that it provides a partial solution to this problem by providing a comprehensive overview of available experts. Using a single, centrally organized and funded[33] register has another advantage. It makes it easier to assess the quality of experts because they are all held to the same standards. This counteracts much of the criticism encountered in literature pertaining to the existence of an abundance of different registers judges can choose from in the field of civil law.[34] A problem with the use of a register is that it might *de facto* shift the responsibility for assessing the qualifications of an expert from the judge to the organization in charge of registration.[35] The minister of justice stated that this is not the purpose of the Order. The minister also stated that the fact that an expert meets the requirements of the register does not automatically mean that the expert is in fact the right person to answer the specific question at hand.[36] This reservation on behalf of the minister is justified and also points us to another, more general weakness of the use of a register. The register only sets minimum standards which an expert must meet. Therefore the registration of an expert provides only limited information about his qualifications and says nothing about these qualifications in comparison to other registered experts.[37] Several authors even point out that the best and most brilliant scientists might not want to be included in a register because the limited and

---

28 ECHR 15th of June 2010, 34334/04, (Ashot Haratyunyan/Armenia).
29 ECHR 27th of July 2006, 5010/04, (Hoffen/Liechtenstein).
30 Harris, O'Boyle & Warbrick/Harris et al. 2014, p. 430-431; Mole & Harby 2006, p. 49.
31 Ovey &White 2002, p. 158; ECHR 19th of April 1994, 16034/90, (Van de Hurk/The Netherlands).
32 Letter from the Dutch minister of justice to the royal dutch academy of science: <https://zoek.officielebekendmakingen.nl/kst-31116-E-b1.pdf>; Van Dijk 2009.
33 Akkermans points out that the independence and impartiality of a publically funded register is better guaranteed then in the case of a (partly) privately funded register which is common in Dutch civil and administrative law. A.J. Akkermans as cited in: Evenblij 2008, p. 66.
34 See for instance: Evenblij 2008; Van Spaendonck & Keijser 2014.
35 The judiciary itself seems to be aware of this risk: Keulen et al. 2010, p. 111.
36 NvT 2009, 330, p. 19.
37 Similarly: De Ridder *et al.* 2014, p. 78.

common information included in such a register will prevent them from distinguishing themselves from their less talented colleagues.[38] Whether or not these concerns are justified remains unclear. Recent evaluation of the register does show that due to the focus on minimum standards, so-called super-specialists[39] are not (and might never be) included in the register. The same applies to experts in (very) small fields of expertise.[40] Article 16 sub c of the Order provides the possibility to have specific skills, such as experience with specific research methods, included in the register. Evaluation of the register shows that this option is not being used in practice.[41] In my opinion, this problem can be partly overcome by article 511 sub 1 CCP, which is a codification of a judgment of the Dutch Supreme Court in 1998.[42] It requires the expert to deliver a detailed report including information on the research method used as well as the reliability of that method. The expert is subsequently required to provide information on his personal skills in using that particular research method. Where the requirements of a register are by default common[43] the information required by article 511 CCP is specifically relevant to the case at hand. The provision provides the expert with the possibility to provide a judge, the defence or the public prosecution with more recent, relevant information which does not belong to the (minimum) requirements to be included in the register.[44] Although this information cannot influence the initial choice for a specific expert as the additional information will only be available upon completion of the report, it allows the judge, as well as the defence and the public prosecution, to assess, *ex post* the choice for that particular expert.[45] If at that point the judge still has doubts concerning the accuracy of the advice or the qualifications of the expert he can decide to appoint another expert[46] on the basis of article 315 sub 3 CCP.

---

[38] The royal Dutch academy of science expressed its fears that only scientists with 'limited capabilities' will end up being included in the register: <www.eerstekamer.nl/behandeling/20081007/brief_van_de_knaw_van_30_juli_2008/document3/f=/w31116dbijl2.pdf>; Similarly: N.J.M. Kwakman, 'De wet deskundige in strafzaken: Een remmende sprong vooruit?', *Ars Aequi* 2011, 4, p. 310-311>.

[39] Highly specialized experts in a subarea of a field of expertise.

[40] De Ridder *et al.* 2014, p. 77.

[41] De Ridder *et al.* 2014, p. 68 and 89.

[42] Hoge Raad (Supreme Court) 27th of Januari 1998, ECLI:NL:HR:1998:ZD0917, *Nederlandse Jurisprudentie* 1998, 404, with annotation J.M. Reijntjes (Schoenmakers-arrest); *Kamerstukken II* 2006/07, 31 116, nr. 3, p. 7 en 24; Hielkema 2009, p. 32-33.

[43] Kwakman 2011, p. 311.

[44] The period during which the registration is valid is regulated by article 17 of the Order and is set to four years; On the risks of a (too) long period of registration without re-evaluation: Derksen 2010, p. 538.

[45] Positive prior experience with an expert might lead to this expert being appointed more often: Keulen *et al.* 2010, p. 110. In that case I believe a more than averagely talented expert can distinguish himself from others.

[46] The appointment of more than one expert will be further examined in paragraph 6.

One of the characteristics of Dutch criminal law is that most experts are appointed prior to the actual trial. Prior to the court session, experts can be appointed by a pre-trial examining judge and the public prosecution service on the basis of article 150b and 227 CCP or article 150 and 150a CCP respectively. This means that the trial judge, who is exclusively responsible for assessing the quality of the expert (findings), has no influence on the actual appointment. This is especially problematic in the case of experts that are appointed by the public prosecution service.[47] Van Kempen points out that in Dutch criminal proceedings the pre-trial stage seems to become increasingly important in favor of the actual trial stage.[48] This adds a layer of responsibility for the public prosecution service to safeguard the interests of the defence. In Van Kempen's (and my) opinion the emphasis on the pre-trial stage poses the risk of the public prosecution becoming less magisterial and more of a partial opponent to the defence.[49] In my opinion the trial judge has to take this into consideration when assessing the reliability and accuracy of the expert advice.

In several judgments the ECHR acknowledged and condoned the fact that the advice of a court appointed expert can be expected to carry more weight than that of an otherwise appointed expert.[50] Although it seems only logical to ascribe a similar weight to reports by experts who are listed in a register specifically designed to be used in criminal proceedings, I have found no indication in practice that Dutch judges are inclined to do so.[51]

One of the main rationales of using the register is to assist the judge in finding a qualified expert. This is important for two reasons. First of all there is the logical correlation between the expert, his skills and qualifications, and the quality of the expert report.[52] Secondly it has been pointed out in literature that judges in general only perform a superficial check of expert reports.[53] This makes the initial choice for the '*right*' expert even more important. Given the fact that the register does not include the most qualified experts for at least some of the questions at hand, the so-called super-specialists, I believe that the main advantage of a register lies not in

[47] Unless the appointment is at the request of the accused but that happens in only a minority of cases.
[48] Van Kempen 2011, p. 24; This emphasis on the pre-trial stage can also be found in the recent contourennota that serves as a starting point for the upcoming modernization of the Dutch CCP.
[49] Van Kempen 2011, p. 24.
[50] For instance: EHRM 6th of May 1985, 8658/79, *Nederlandse Jurisprudentie* 1989, 385, with annotation P. van Dijk, (Bönisch/Austria).
[51] Which could imply that judges take the fact that most of the registered experts are being appointed by the public prosecution into account.
[52] De Bock 2011, p. 313-314; Verkerk 2008, p. 175-176; Van Spaendonck & Keijser 2014, p. 52.
[53] Van Kempen 2012, p. 110; Verkerk 2010, p. 168.

finding the most qualified expert, but in preventing the selection of an unqualified one.[54] An unqualified expert cannot be expected to produce an accurate and reliable report capable of assisting the judge in finding the truth. The contrary is, in my opinion, less self-evident as such factors like reluctance or carelessness on behalf of the expert or limited research materials can contribute to sub-par results from a well-qualified expert. Which brings us back to where we started: the knowledge gap. The judge has to be well aware of the fact that the choice for a registered expert does not compensate for his own lack of knowledge. The register will at the most provide some guarantees that the expert is capable of providing reliable and accurate information that can assist the judge in finding the truth. The judge has to remain vigilant in ensuring that registration does not substitute for reliability, accuracy or truth.

The conclusion of the foregoing must be that registration is a useful instrument for preventing the selection of unqualified experts, but that its advantages in assessing the facts and finding the truth are limited.

4. The second approach: specialization

As discussed before, one of the main issues in dealing with expert evidence is the knowledge gap. This lack of specialized knowledge within the judiciary creates the necessity for expert involvement and subsequently prevents the judge from adequately assessing the reliability and accuracy of the information provided by the expert. The most direct solution to this problem is to ensure that sufficient specialized knowledge becomes available within the judiciary. This can be achieved by way of specialization of judges or by making use of (forensic) experts employed directly by the judiciary.

Specialization within the judiciary is a subject that has caught the attention of authors,[55] politics[56] and the judiciary itself.[57] In recent years the judiciary board, in conjunction with the training and study centre for the judiciary have evaluated and adjusted the training program for members of the judiciary.[58] This training program now emphasizes more than before the importance of non-legal subjects like forensic expertise.[59] The question is, however, whether such education is capable of turning

[54] Similar: De Ridder *et al.* 2014, p. 13, 82, 89-90.
[55] For instance: Jurgens 2012, p. 128-131; Havinga & Neelis 2013.
[56] *Kamerstukken II* 2011/12, 29 279, nr. 148.
[57] Agenda van de rechtspraak 2011-2014; Havinga, Klaassen & Neelis 2012.
[58] Based, among others, on: Van Dam 2008.
[59] www.ssr.nl/index.php?page=alias-25&hl=nl_NL; Also see: *Kamerstukken II* 2009/10,

judges into experts. In my opinion the answer is no. Scientific fields of expertise are rapidly progressing and I believe it to be impossible to educate judges in such a way for them to be able to keep up with that.[60] It has been suggested that judges don't need to have more than mere superficial knowledge in order to be able to assess expert advice.[61] I believe, however, that it makes more sense to educate experts in basic legal knowledge[62] than to educate judges in a sheer infinite number of rapidly evolving fields of expertise. Research suggests that, apart from a lack of knowledge, one of the problems with assessing expert evidence might be a communication problem between judges and experts.[63] Judges and experts seem to think that they understand each other while in fact in quite a number of cases they actually don't. This might lead to the misuse of expert reports and could subsequently lead to wrongful convictions or acquittals.[64] One of the main steps that has to be taken to solve this problem is to create awareness of this problem among judges and experts, rather than simply improving the judges' knowledge.[65]

A second option might be for the judiciary to employ their own experts or make use of an expert-judge. In recent years some Dutch courts have been experimenting with making use of forensic experts employed directly by the judiciary.[66] These 'in-house' experts are responsible for helping the judges to interpret forensic evidence provided by external experts.

The use of an expert-judge is another way to increase the available expert knowledge within the judiciary. In the Dutch legal system expert-judges are used in the penitentiary court[67] and the military court.[68]

My main concern with the use of 'in-house' experts or expert-judges is that there are no guarantees whatsoever that their expert knowledge leads to more accurate, reliable or truthful results. Because of the knowledge gap, other judges will lack the knowledge to assess the opinion of the expert-judge and therefore have little

---

32 123 VI, nr. 108, p. 3.

[60] Similarly, member of parliament Berndsen: *Kamerstukken II* 2011/12, 29 279, nr. 139, p. 14; Moraal has also stated that this is in fact impossible: Moraal 2007, p. 37.

[61] Derksen 2010, p. 536-537.

[62] This is already one of the requirements of the register.

[63] De Keijser *et al.* 2009.

[64] Brants points to a 2008 study suggesting expert evidence plays a part in an increasing number of wrongful convictions: Huff & Killias 2008; Brants 2012, p. 12.

[65] De Keijser *et al.* 2009, p. 69-70.

[66] An evaluation of this pilot can be found at: <www.rechtspraak.nl/Organisatie-en-contact/Organisatie/Raad-voor-de-rechtspraak/Nieuws/Documents/(256140063)%20EVALUATIE%20PILOT%20FORENSISHE%20ONDERSTEUNING%20).pdf>.

[67] Article 67 of the Judiciary act.

[68] Article 55 of the Judiciary act.

alternative than to rely on it. This is particularly troublesome as it can be expected that, similar to that of a court appointed expert,[69] the assessment of the evidence report by an expert-judge will carry significant weight. Another problem of 'promoting' an expert to the status of judge is that it may have a negative effect on the adversarial debate in court.[70] The right to adversarial proceedings derives directly from the right to a fair trial as guaranteed by article 6 ECHR.[71] Part of this right for the defendant is:

'the opportunity [...] to [...] comment on all evidence adduced or observations filed with a view to influencing the court's decision.'[72]

Because the observations of the expert-judge pertaining to an expert report are not communicated to the defendant[73] he is unable to respond to it.[74] This seriously impairs the adversarial debate. The use of expert-judges is, however, in accordance with article 6 ECHR as long as the tribunal 'as a whole' can be considered 'an independent and impartial tribunal established by law'.[75] The case of Bönisch v Austria illustrates where there may be a problem. In that case the ECHR concluded that there had been a breach of the right to equality of arms, based on, *inter alia*, the following reasoning:

'The Court considers [...] that such equal treatment had not been afforded in the two proceedings in issue.[...] various circumstances illustrate the dominant role that the Director was enabled to play. In his capacity of ''expert'', he could attend throughout the hearings, put questions to the accused and to witnesses with the leave of the court and comment on their evidence at the appropriate moment. The lack of equal treatment was particularly striking in the first proceedings, by reason of the difference between the respective positions of the court expert and the ''expert witness'' of the defence. [...] Consequently, there has been a breach of Article 6 para. 1'[76]

---

[69] De Roos 2007, p. 4.
[70] Similarly, member of parliament Recourt: *Kamerstukken II* 2011/12, 29 279, nr. 139, p. 14; Buruma 2006, p. 18; De Groot-van Leeuwen & Van Steenbergen 2006, p. 48.
[71] ECHR 23rd of June 1993, 12952/87, (Ruiz-Mateos/Spain), r.o. 63.
[72] ECHR 8th of August 2006 , 43803/98, *NJCM-Bulletin* 2007, p. 697-706, with annotation P. van Dijk, (Eskelinen et al./Finland), r.o. 31; Also see: ECHR 18th of February 1997, 18990/91, (Nideröst-Huber/Switserland); ECHR 18th of March 1997, 21497/93, *Nederlandse Jurisprudentie* 1998, 278, with annotation H.J. Snijders, (Mantovanelli/France).
[73] The deliberation in the judges' chambers is bound by secrecy according to article 7 sub 3 of the Judiciary act.
[74] More on this subject in paragraph 6.
[75] As indicated the use of expert-judges is regulated by law so this should not pose a problem.
[76] ECHR 6th of May 1985, 8658/79, *Nederlandse Jurisprudentie* 1989, 385, with annotation P. van Dijk, (Bönisch/Austria), *r.o. 33-35.*

Would this particular expert not have been an appointed expert but in fact an expert-judge I believe the previous quote would not have posed a problem for the ECHR as an expert-judge is well within his rights to put questions to parties and comment on the evidence behind closed doors. This example illustrates that the way in which an expert is viewed upon is, among other factors, influenced by his formal position. Research shows that external experts are almost never appointed in courts in which expert-judges take part,[77] thus making it appear as if the need for expert knowledge and the knowledge gap have disappeared. This effect, however, is mere window-dressing, disguising the problem of the knowledge gap rather than solving it.

5. The third approach: adversarial debate

The third and last possible approach to ensure the accuracy of expert evidence is to create an adversarial debate. Although the right to adversarial proceedings derives directly from the right to a fair trial as guaranteed by article 6 ECHR,[78] this article does not include the right to a counter-expert under all circumstances. It merely guarantees parties the right to effectively comment on the expert advice.[79] In the Netherlands, the rights of accused to a counter-expert are guaranteed well beyond the minimum standard set by article 6 ECHR. The Dutch court of cassation ruled that an accused, under a few strict conditions,[80] has the right to counter-expertise. Articles 150a sub 3, 151a sub 6 and 231 sub 1 CCP provide an opportunity for the defence to request a counter-expertise as well.[81] Recent research suggests that the use of more than one expert, and the adversarial debate that derives from that, leads to a more thorough examination of the expert evidence.[82] The question remains, however, whether a more thorough examination of the expert evidence leads to a better assessment of the accuracy because the knowledge gap may still pose a problem in this regard. In general it can be stated that, notwithstanding the knowledge gap, if several experts agree amongst each other, this increases the validity of the information. If, however, expert opinions are contradictory, this should highlight to the judge specific points that need further scrutiny. The attentive reader might notice we risk getting trapped in a vicious circle here since the

[77] Böcker *et al* 2010, p. 314.
[78] ECHR 23rd of June 1993, 12952/87, (Ruiz-Mateos/Spain), r.o. 63.
[79] ECHR 18th of march 1997, 21497/93, *Nederlandse Jurisprudentie* 1998, 278, with annotation H.J. Snijders, (Mantovanelli/France).
[80] Hoge Raad (Supreme Court) 13rd May 1997, ECLI:NL:HR:1997:ZD0705, *Nederlandse Jurisprudentie* 1998, 152; More detailed on this: Hielkema 1999, p. 33-34.
[81] And of course it is also possible for the defence to hire their own expert.
[82] Rijnsburger & Malsch 2013, p. 6.

knowledge gap will probably still prevent the judge from assessing the accuracy of those points the experts do not agree on. An additional problem that pertains to truth finding is that it may well be possible that two contrary opinions of experts are both scientifically valid.[83] This might not be a problem though, because the task of the judge is not to assess the accuracy of the expert report in itself, but to assess the accuracy of the expert report in the light of all the available evidence.

A multitude of different solutions as to what to do with contrary opinions from experts have been suggested by different authors,[84] some of which are actually applied abroad.[85] Although creating an adversarial debate between experts does not solve the problem created by the knowledge gap and therefore has its limitations in helping the judge in his search for the truth I do believe that it is an indispensable tool for a judge to assess the accuracy of expert evidence.[86] A major advantage of creating an adversarial debate among experts is that they can help assess the accuracy of each other's findings. This does not change the fact that the judge remains responsible for the final assessment. I can therefore see no harm in, *de facto*, delegating some of that responsibility to the experts.

In paragraph four I mentioned article 511 sub 1 CCP. This provision requires the expert to provide information on the research method, the reliability of the method and to what extent he is personally skilled in using that method. The information thus provided can be used as a starting point for an adversarial debate. Aside from pointing out weaknesses in the qualifications of the expert, the judge seeking to stimulate an adversarial debate can for instance use the provided information to specifically select a counter-expert who is known for using a different research method.

6. Conclusion

We are living in an ever more complex society in which technique and science are constantly evolving. As scientific developments are getting more and more incorporated into everyday aspects of our lives, it is not surprising that their influence will increasingly be felt in criminal proceedings. Although the actual nature of many criminal offences may not change, the interpretation of the

---

[83] Van Kempen 2012, p. 111.
[84] For an (not exhaustive) overview see: Van Kempen 2012, p. 111-112.
[85] For instance the 'prehearing discussion of expert evidence' as used in England (article 33.6 of The Criminal Procedure Rules).
[86] Similar: Brants 2012, p. 18; Rijnsburger & Malsch 2013, p. 6.

underlying facts becomes more complex.[87] Because expert knowledge now covers a large part of the facts that are relevant to a judge in assessing the guilt of an accused person, it becomes increasingly necessary to obtain the advice of experts as they are most qualified to assist in finding the truth. The paradox in this is that by consulting more experts the judge is likely to have more accurate facts at his disposal while at the same time the increasingly complex nature of those facts will make it ever so hard to assess them properly.

This is put into perspective when, first of all, one realizes that, as mentioned earlier, assessing the accuracy of expert evidence is not the sole purpose of the judiciary. The judge has to assess all available evidence including the expert evidence in light of the legal question at hand. Secondly it has been the main argument of this contribution that the knowledge gap can be partly compensated.

Article 6 ECHR is of little consequence to the three suggested approaches, apart maybe from the lack of adversarial debate caused by the involvement of expert-judges in criminal proceedings. We have seen that all of the three approaches comply with the minimum standards set by article 6 ECHR. While none of the approaches provides certainty about the accuracy or truthfulness of an expert report, they may all be helpful in establishing the truth. Their contribution lies mainly in preventing mistakes and pointing out possible weaknesses, thereby reducing the chance that a judge relies on questionable information.

To counteract the consequences of the knowledge gap the judge has no other choice than to depend on external advice. As argued above the second approach is least suitable for assessing the accuracy of expert evidence.[88] The best results will derive from a combination of the first and third approaches.

The relation between appointing the right expert and getting the most accurate expert advice is obvious and needs no further explanation. The first approach can serve as a useful starting point in the search for the right expert. A register that sets and maintains high enough standards will at least weed out underqualified experts thereby limiting the search for the right expert to a (relatively) select number. The register might not be able to counteract the problem that the most qualified experts in certain fields of expertise are not included in the register. It can, however, do

---

[87] Hitting a person with a baseball bat is still the same as it was a hundred years ago but the science pertaining to the psyche of the offender as well as the possibility to obtain all sorts of information from trace evidence left on the bat has changed significantly. The fact that 'every contact leaves a trace' is not new, but dates back to Locard's 'exchange principle': Locard 1934. The quantity and quality of information that can be obtained from trace evidence has however increased over the years.
[88] Similar: Brants 2012, p. 18; There are authors who do believe in the second approach, for instance: Derksen 2010, p. 534-557.

more than simply register experts that meet the minimum requirements. As pointed out above the existing possibility to include more detailed information on skills or specific research methods is not being used in practice. In paragraph four I mentioned article 511 sub 1 CCP. This provision requires the expert to include in his report information on the research method, the reliability of the method and to what extent he is personally skilled in using that method. It is that kind of information that I would like to see included in the register. Given the fact that the expert is required to provide this information anyway on completion of a report I believe this can serve as a good starting point for collecting information to be included in the register.[89] The advantage is that the availability, up front, of specific information regarding the skills of specific experts allows for a more custom selection of experts which would in general be beneficial for the (expected) accuracy of their advice. Since judges all suffer from the knowledge gap they might not be the ideal candidates to make this selection. Perhaps what is also needed is a more active role for the organization that is responsible for maintaining the register in selecting the right expert to answer a specific question.[90]

According to Brants judges are legal professionals but will always remain layman with regard to the contents of an expert advice.[91] What judges can do is see to it that others ask the questions they are unable to ask. Creating an adversarial debate lies well within their possibilities. A judge can supervise such a debate and make sure it focusses on the issues that are relevant to the legal question at hand. Making use of a register ensures that the selected expert can reasonably be expected to provide accurate reports. In a similar vein an adversarial debate reduces the chance of a judge drawing conclusions based on inaccurate advice. If more experts agree on certain conclusions, their findings may be regarded as, to use a legal term, 'beyond a reasonable doubt'. Where judges become aware of existing disagreement between experts they should, whilst being mindful of the knowledge gap, take this into consideration while weighing all the available evidence including the expert report. Maybe this *de facto* shifts the task of examining the accuracy of expert advice from the judge to the experts but this is in my opinion inevitable and also does not change the fact that the judge remains responsible for the final assessment.

---

[89] The register does not include specific skills and qualifications because, in the opinion of the organization behind the register, they require (too) complex supplementary norms and tests: De Ridder *et al.* 2014, p. 78.

[90] That role now (partly) falls to the Netherlands forensic institute (NFI) and the Institute for forensic psychiatry and psychology (NIFP): De Ridder *et al.* 2014, p. 89. These organizations are also not ideal candidates since they both employ experts and questions might arise concerning their independence.

[91] Brants 2012, p. 18.

Both the first and third approach involve external influences on the judges' assessment of the accuracy of expert advice. I don't think this devaluates or excuses the judge from his own responsibility to draw conclusions based on, *inter alia*, the expert advice. His responsibilities are to create the ideal circumstances for the realization of an accurate expert advice and to weigh the evidence. If the expert advice, in spite of measures taken to assure an accurate and reliable outcome, is still open to interpretation it is the responsibility of the judge to draw conclusions and act upon them. As argued by Van Kempen a judge needs to prevent making an arbitrary choice between two or more expert advices that he does not fully comprehend.[92] In such cases a judge has to either seek additional (expert) information or decide not to use the expert report at all.

[92] Van Kempen 2012, p. 111.

Bibliography

Abma 1956

K. Abma, *Deskundigen,* Wageningen: N.V. Gebr. Zomer & Keunings Uitgeversmij 1956.

De Bock 2011

R.H. de Bock, *Tussen waarheid en onzekerheid: Over het vaststellen van feiten in de civiele procedure* (diss. Tilburg), Deventer: Kluwer 2011.

Böcker et al. 2010

A. Böcker et al., *Specialisatie loont?! Ervaringen van grote ondernemingen met specialistische rechtspraakvoorzieningen,* Den Haag: Sdu 2010.

Brants 2012

C.H. Brants, 'Tegenspraak als vereiste van waarheidsvinding en eerlijk proces bij vingerafdrukbewijs', *Expertise en Recht* 2012, 1.

Buruma 2006

Y. Buruma, 'Concentratie en specialisatie: een inleidende beschouwing', in: J.W.M. Tromp *et al.* (eds.), *Concentratie en specialisatie van rechtspraak: noodzaak of overbodig?,* Deventer: Kluwer 2006, p. 18.

Buruma 2009

Y. Buruma, 'Betrouwbaar bewijs', *DD* 2009, 23.

Cleiren 2001

C.P.M. Cleiren, 'Waarheid in het strafrecht: Niet tot elke prijs', in: C.P.M. Cleiren, R.H. de Bock & C.J.M. Klaassen, *Het procesrecht en de waarheidsvinding,* Den Haag: Boom juridische uitgevers 2001.

Cleiren 2008

C.P.M. Cleiren, 'Monopolie op strafrechtelijke waarheidsvinding. Overwegingen over belang en risico's van private ''deskundigen''-inbreng', *Strafblad* 2008, 3.

Crijns 2008

J.H. Crijns, 'Een kroniek van de strafrechtelijke waarheidsvinding', in: J.H. Crijns, P.P.J. van der Meij & J.M. ten Voorde (eds.), *De waarde van waarheid. Opstellen over waarheid en waarheidsvinding in het strafrecht*, Den Haag: Boom juridische uitgevers 2008.

Crijns, Van der Meij & Ten Voorde 2010

J.H. Crijns, P.P.M. van der Meij & J.M. ten Voorde, 'Forensisch onderzoek voor ''dummies''. Hoe leren de deskundige en de strafrechter elkaar te verstaan?', *Ars Aequi* juli/augustus 2010.

Van Dam 2008

P.C.T. van Dam (ed.), *De strafrechter en profil: deskundigheidsbevordering van de strafrechter,* Den Haag: Raad voor de rechtspraak 2008.

Derksen 2010

A.A. Derksen, 'Het duivels dilemma van de deskundige of een alledaags probleem', *Strafblad* 2010, p. 538.

Van Dijk 2009

Chr.H. van Dijk, 'De te stellen eisen aan deskundigen en de noodzaak van een openbaar landelijk register voor alle rechtsgebieden', *Expertise en recht* 2009, 5/6.

Dubelaar & Nijboer 2008

M.J. Dubelaar & J.F. Nijboer, 'De procespositie van deskundigen eindelijk wettelijk verankerd', *DD* 2008, 2.

Evenblij 2008

M. Evenblij,'Gerechtelijk deskundigen. Vechten tegen de kennisparadox', Mr. Magazine 2008, 6/7.

De Groot 2012

G. de Groot, 'Waarheidsvinding in het civiele (proces)recht', in: *Waarheid en waarheidsvinding in het recht* (Handelingen Nederlandse juristen-vereniging 2012-1), Deventer: Kluwer 2012.

De Groot & Akkermans 2007

G. de Groot & A.J. Akkermans, 'Schadevaststelling, bewijslastverdeling en deskundigenbericht', *NTBR* 2007.

De Groot-van leeuwen & Van Steenbergen 2006

L.E. de Groot-van Leeuwen & S. van Steenbergen, 'Specialistische rechtspraak in de ogen van rechters en wetenschappers', in: J.W.M. Tromp et al. (eds.), *Concentratie en specialisatie van rechtspraak: noodzaak of overbodig?,* Deventer: Kluwer 2006.

Harris, O'Boyle & Warbrick/ Harris et al. 2014

Harris, O'Boyle & Warbrick/D.J. Harris et al., *Law of the European convention on human rights,* Oxford: Oxford University Press 2014.

Den Hartog 2005

J.D. den Hartog, 'De selectie en waardering van bewijsmateriaal', in: A. Harteveld, D.H. de Jong & E. Stamhuis (eds.), *Systeem in ontwikkeling. Liber Amicorum G. Knigge,* Nijmegen: Wolf Legal Publishers 2005.

Havinga & Neelis 2013

T. Havinga & M. Neelis, 'Specialisatie gewenst voor IT-zaken? Een broncode? Nog nooit van gehoord.', *Nijmegen Sociology of law working papers series* 2013-02.

Havinga, Klaassen & Neelis 2012

T. Havinga, C.J.M. Klaassen & N. Neelis, *Specialisatie gewenst? De behoefte aan gespecialiseerde rechtspraak binnen het Nederlandse bedrijfsleven,* Den Haag, Raad voor de rechtspraak 2012.

Hielkema 1999

J. Hielkema, 'Experts in Dutch criminal procedures', in: M. Malsch & J.F. Nijboer (eds.), *Complex cases: Perspectives on the Netherlands criminal justice system,* Amsterdam: Thela Thesis, 1999.

Hielkema 2009

J. Hielkema, 'Wet deskundige in strafzaken', *Ontmoetingen* 2009, nr. 15.

Huff & Killias 2008

C.R. Huff & M. Killias (eds.), *Wrongful Conviction. International Perspective on Miscarriages of Justice*, Philadelphia: Temple university press 2008.

Jurgens 2012

M. Jurgens, 'De vakgebiedspecialist in fraudezaken', *Strafblad* 2012, 2.

De Keijser 2009

J.W. de Keijser *et al.*, *Bijkans begrepen? Feitelijk en vermeend begrip van forensische deskundigenrapportages onder rechters, advocaten en deskundigen,* Den Haag: Boom juridische uitgevers 2009.

Van Kempen 2011

P.H.P.H.M.C. van Kempen, 'Verdedigingsrechten in het vooronderzoek in Nederland', *Strafblad* 2011, 2.

Van Kempen 2012

P.H.P.H.M.C. van Kempen, 'Risico's aan deskundigenonderzoek- Hoe kan de strafrechter zijn onafhankelijkheid en taakuitoefening waarborgen?', *Strafblad* 2012, 2.

Keulen 2010

B.F. Keulen *et al.*, *Het deskundigenregister in strafzaken,* Den Haag: Boom juridische uitgevers 2010.

Kwakman 2014

N.J.M. Kwakman, 'De illusie van de materiële waarheid en de houdbaarheid van de doelstelling van de materiële waarheidsvinding in het strafproces', *Strafblad* 2014, 6.

De Lange 2012

A. de Lange, 'De externe werking van het deskundigenregister', *Strafblad* 2012, 2.

Locard 1934

E. Locard, *La police et les méthode scientifique,* Paris: Editions Rieder 1934.

Mackor 2010

A.R. Mackor, 'Wat is waarheid? De rol van deskundigen bij waarheidsvinding in de strafrechtspraak', *Netherlands journal of legal philosophy* 2010, 1.

Middelbos & Smithuis 2008

N.J. Middelbos & M.M.A. Smithuis, 'Nederlands register gerechtelijk deskundigen', *Expertise en recht* 2008, 3.

Mole & Harby 2006

N. Mole & C. Harby, *The right to a fair trial. Human rights handbook, No. 3,* Strasbourg: Directorate general of human rights council of Europe 2006.

Moraal 2007

H.J. Moraal, 'Specialisatie bij zittende en staande magistratuur, advocatuur en deskundigen', in: H. Elffers & M.A.J. Elzinga (eds.), *Deskundige behandeling van deskundigen. Het gebruik van deskundigenrapportages in de rechtszaal,* Rapport NSCR 2007, 3.

Nijboer 1993

J.F. Nijboer, 'Het streven naar de materiële waarheid in het strafproces', in: M. Hildebrand et al., Een *afzonderlijke procedure voor de bekennende verdachte?*, Arnhem: Gouda Quint 1993.

Nijboer 2011

J.F. Nijboer, *Strafrechtelijk bewijsrecht,* Nijmegen: Ars Aequi Libri 2011.

Ovey & White 2002

C. Ovey & R. White, *Jacobs and White, The European convention on human rights,* New York: Oxford University Press 2002.

De Ridder et al. 2014

J. de Ridder et al., *Evaluatie van het Nederlands Register Gerechtelijk Deskundigen,* Groningen: Pro Facto 2014.

Rijnsburger & Malsch 2013

M.D. Rijnsburger & M. Malsch, 'Toetsing door de rechter van deskundigenbewijs. Is er voldoende tegenspraak?', *Expertise en Recht* 2013, 1.

De Roos 2007

Th.A. de Roos, 'Perikelen rond deskundigen', in: H. Elffers & M.A.J. Elzinga (eds.), *Deskundige behandeling van deskundigen. Het gebruik van deskundigenrapportages in de rechtszaal,* Rapport NSCR 2007, 3, p. 4.

Van Spaendonck & Keijser 2014

Ph.M. van Spaendonck & N.M. Keijser, 'Kwaliteitswaarborging van deskundigenberichten in het civiel recht', *Trema* februari 2014.

Verkerk 2008

R. Verkerk, 'Procesrechtelijke waarborgen voor een betrouwbaar deskundigenonderzoek', in: G.C. Hesen et al. (eds.), *Schadevaststelling en de rol van de deskundige,* Deventer: Kluwer 2008.

Verkerk 2010

R.R. Verkerk, *Fact-finding in civil litigation* (diss. Maastricht), Antwerpen: Intersentia 2010.

Ten Voorde 2008

J.M. ten Voorde, 'In- en uitleiding', in: J.H. Crijns, P.P.J. van der Meij & J.M. ten Voorde (eds.), *De waarde van waarheid. Opstellen over waarheid en waarheidsvinding in het strafrecht,* Den Haag: Boom juridische uitgevers 2008.

De Vries 2002

G.H. de Vries, 'Wat is waarheid? Een filosofische benadering', *Justitiële verkenningen* 2002, 2.

Dealing with dictators: the importance of interdisciplinary research when addressing complex criminality

Maartje Weerdesteijn[1]

Introduction

International crimes, meaning genocide, crimes against humanity and war crimes are addressed in an environment where political and legal considerations are intricately woven together. The complex nature of these crimes makes answering questions about how to counter them particularly difficult. The present research will deal with situations in which international crimes are perpetrated in non-democratic regimes by the state against its own population. Although international crimes are perpetrated by different regimes in a variety of circumstances, several scholars have come to the conclusion that these crimes are particularly prevalent in authoritarian regimes.[2] When the state is the perpetrator of these crimes this sets the conventional system on its head. Usually the state is an inhibiting factor that keeps the prevalence of crimes in check, however, often in authoritarian regimes the crimes may be legitimated by the state, and the state comes to incite rather than control them.[3] In those situations, the non-democratic leader often propagates an ideology which may act as a justification and rationalisation for the crimes.[4] In flagrant disregard for their obligations to protect their own populations from these core crimes, the state is often the instigator and no serious policies to stop or mitigate their occurrence may therefore be expected from the government of such a state.

While it has been widely recognised in different treaties and customary law[5] that states have the obligation to protect their own population from international crimes,

[1] Maartje Weerdesteijn is a PhD candidate at Tilburg University.
[2] Rummel 1994; Fein 1995; Krain 2000; Kreutz 2006; Harff 2003; Bellamy & McLoughlin 2009; Regan & Henderson 2002. Pinker highlights the other side of the coin and argues that democracy turned out 'to be one of the greatest violence reduction technologies since the appearance of government itself', Pinker 2011, p. 161.
[3] Haveman & Smeulers 2008, 6-7; Alvarez 2001, 56-85.
[4] Alvarez 2001, p. 69, 79; Alvarez 2008, p. 217; Chirot & McCauley 2010, p. 65-69; Woolf & Hulsizer 2005, p. 103-108; Staub 2010, p. 173.
[5] Convention on the Prevention and Punishment of the Crime of Genocide, Geneva Conventions, on the customary law status of the prohibition on genocide see for instance most

in 2005 states established that they also have a responsibility to protect which extends beyond their borders.[6] At the 2005 World Summit states accepted the responsibility to help other states live up to the responsibility to protect their population from genocide, war crimes, ethnic cleansing and crimes against humanity, and when they manifestly failed to do so, voiced their preparedness to act collectively.[7] The implementation of the Responsibility to Protect (R2P), however, leaves much to be desired.[8]

It will be argued here that while the dictator plays an important part in bringing these crimes about, not all dictators are alike and this needs to be taken into account since the success of foreign policy measures targeted at mitigating or stopping these atrocities may depend on the responsiveness of the dictator. Analysing how the responsiveness of different dictators may impact the success of these foreign policy measures requires a scholar to investigate many different fields of study which previously largely developed in isolation of each other. Not only is it important that the causes of international crimes are investigated, as well as the role the dictator plays therein, but also the responsiveness of the dictatorial leader to foreign policy mechanisms needs to be assessed. This requires an approach in which many different fields of study are combined. International criminology may provide for an overarching framework as it is not determined by disciplinary boundaries, but is guided by its subject matter and because of that is inherently interdisciplinary.

In the analysis that follows, such an interdisciplinary study is undertaken in which the dictator takes centre stage. Despite the important role that dictators are said to play in international crimes, and despite the tremendous decision making power that dictatorial leaders have in their country, no research has yet been done that investigates how foreign policy making can become more effective when it acknowledges that there are differences in the responsiveness of dictators when they orchestrate the perpetration of international crimes.[9] Much of the research in the different fields has been developed without scholars looking beyond their own discipline but as will be argued here, bringing them together can provide valuable

---

recently ICJ *Application of the Convention on the Prevention and Punishment of the Crime of Genocide* (Croatia v. Serbia), 2015.

[6] '2005 World Summit Outcome', United Nations: General Assembly, 2005. A/RES/60/1; Stahn 2007.

[7] '2005 World Summit Outcome', A/RES/60/1.

[8] Havel & Tutu 2012, p. 85.

[9] Although some work exists that draws lessons for foreign policy from studying the personality of individual leaders (e.g Post 2004), these involve in depth case studies of single leaders and do not create a more general distinction between different kinds of leaders with corresponding foreign policy implications. A more general differentiation was made with respect to *regime types* and the *strategies* of leaders, but these do not focus on the personal characteristics of the dictator. For an overview see Ezrow & Frantz 2011.

insights that should be kept in mind when addressing these particular forms of complex criminality. The goal is not to sweep differences between the disciplines under the rug, but to highlight the unique focus of each discipline and point out the ways in which they can learn from each other.

Firstly, a legal analysis will assess what the responsibilities and obligations are of states to protect their own populations and those in other countries from falling victim to international crimes. Thereafter, it will be explained how these efforts can be made more effective by taking into account the role the dictator plays in bringing the crimes about, and taking the differences between dictators into consideration when devising responses to these crimes. A new perspective will be provided that suggests that acknowledging the differences between dictators that either use the ideology instrumentally, or are genuinely committed to the belief system they put forward, may have important implications for the prevention and mitigation of these crimes.

1. Law: Extent of legal obligations

At the 2005 World Summit, countries accepted they had the Responsibility to Protect their own population, and those of other states, from genocide, war crimes, ethnic cleansing and crimes against humanity. It was a landmark moment for the Responsibility to Protect in which the concept became formally accepted by the international community. The formulation of the concept in the Outcome Document was much more limited than the manner in which it was developed in its original report but it was a great accomplishment that consensus could be achieved on such a contentious concept that touches on the very core of a state's sovereignty.[10]

The Secretary General of the United Nations would later explain in his report that he saw the responsibility as agreed to at the summit as resting on three pillars. Countries not only accepted that they carried the responsibility to protect their own populations from atrocities, pillar one, but also to help other nations live up to these responsibilities, pillar two, and finally in pillar three, when states manifestly fail to

[10] The outcome document is much more limited than the original report because it makes no mention of what should be done when the Security Council is deadlocked, does not specify any criteria for military action and ignores the responsibility to rebuild. Burke-White 2012, p. 27.

do so, agreed they were prepared to take measures collectively to protect the population under threat.[11]

These responsibilities are not all legal obligations and the Responsibility to Protect overall is best seen as a political commitment. This, however, does not mean it is devoid of legal content. It reflects existing legal obligations but the political commitment extends beyond what is codified in law. This has led some scholars to view R2P as potentially laying a foundation for the further development into binding law for those elements that are not binding yet.[12] In order to assess the extent of the legal obligations it is instructive to look at each pillar in turn.

The first pillar is less controversial than the other two. The obligation of a state to ensure that human rights as they are enshrined in many human rights treaties are respected, is well established. These state obligations stem from treaties such as the International Covenant on Civil and Political Rights (ICCPR), Convention on the Prevention and Punishment of the Crime of Genocide (genocide convention), the Convention against Torture and Other Cruel, Inhuman or Degrading Treatment or Punishment (CAT) and the Geneva Conventions but also arises from customary international law.[13] These conventions place obligations upon states and form part of international human rights law and humanitarian law. While these are distinct areas of law, there is an overlap with international criminal law which holds individuals accountable since all violations of the core crimes will also breach rights which are protected in international human rights law or humanitarian law.

State officials can be held accountable through international criminal law for violating these rights when this amounts to a violation of one of the core international crimes. Definitions of genocide, crimes against humanity and war crimes[14] are all incorporated into the statutes of the International Criminal Tribunal for the former Yugoslavia (ICTY), International Criminal Tribunal for Rwanda (ICTR) and the International Criminal Court (ICC) and other international criminal courts and tribunals, and jurisprudence has further delineated the contours of these crimes. Ethnic cleansing can generally be seen to fall under one of the other crimes,

---

[11] Ban 2009.

[12] Brunnee & Toope 2010; Burke-White 2012, p. 23.

[13] On the customary law status of the prohibition on genocide see for instance most recently ICJ *Application of the Convention on the Prevention and Punishment of the Crime of Genocide* (Croatia v. Serbia).
There is not yet a convention on crimes against humanity but efforts to create such a convention are, however, under way. Leila Nadya Sadat, ed. *Forging a Convention for Crimes against Humanity* (Cambridge: Cambridge University Press, 2011).

[14] According to paragraph 139 of the Outcome Document R2P covers ‘genocide, war crimes, ethnic cleansing and crimes against humanity’ and thus mostly overlaps with the core crimes as they have been defined by the ICC with ethnic cleansing often being subsumed under one of the other categories. Chhabra & Zucker 2012 p. 53-54.

depending on the case this can be war crimes, crimes against humanity or genocide, but has no specific legal meaning in itself.[15]

The extent to which pillars two and three also have an obligatory character is much more complicated and controversial. Especially the duties of states regarding crimes against humanity and ethnic cleansing remain unspecified for pillar two and three.[16] The genocide convention and Geneva Conventions provide more guidance. In article 1 of the Geneva Conventions it is stipulated that states should 'undertake to respect *and to ensure respect* for the present Convention in all circumstances' (emphasis my own). Pictet has interpreted this provision to apply 'in the event of a Power failing to fulfil its obligations' and argued that in such circumstances the 'other Contracting Parties (neutral, allied or enemy) may, and should, endeavour to bring it back to an attitude of respect for the convention.'[17]

The genocide convention is also said to entail pillar two and three obligations since article 1 stipulates that states commit themselves to prevent and punish genocide, a provision which extends beyond the state's territorial boundaries.[18] It has, however, long been uncertain what this provision actually means and the extent of the duties it imposes upon states.[19] The judgment in *Bosnia and Hezegovina v. Serbia and Montenegro* was an important step forward in this regard. In its ruling the International Court of Justice found that 'the obligation of States parties is rather to employ all means reasonably available to them, so as to prevent genocide so far as possible.'[20] It was further stipulated that what this entails should be assessed "*in concreto*" with the capacity to influence another state being an important determinant. What states are able to do within the limits of the law was said to depend on the geographical proximity, political ties 'as well as links of all other kinds.'[21] Since geographical proximity is just one of the factors, several scholars have argued it places particular responsibilities on the permanent members of the UN Security Council.[22] They are likely to have the opportunity to do more 'within the limits permitted by international law'[23] considering the influence they have over

---

[15] Chhabra & Zucker 2012, p. 54.
[16] Bellamy & Reike 2010, p. 279.
[17] Pictet 1952, p. 26.
[18] Bischoff, Boas & Reid 2008, p. 151.
[19] Bellamy & Reike 2010, p. 283.
[20] ICJ *Case Concerning Application of the Convention on the Prevention and Punishment of the Crime of Genocide* (Bosnia and Herzegovina v. Serbia and Montenegro), (2007), para. 430.
[21] Ibid.
[22] Glanville 2012, p. 20-24; Arbour 2008, p. 453; Peters 2011.
[23] ICJ *Case Concerning Application of the Convention on the Prevention and Punishment of the Crime of Genocide* (Bosnia and Herzegovina v. Serbia and Montenegro), para 430.

the adoption of particular resolutions and because they are politically powerful actors.[24]

The Secretary General has found that the Security Council carries a moral obligation but some scholars argue that a legal responsibility may also become relevant for either the institution or its individual members.[25] Relying on *Bosnia and Herzegovina v. Serbia and Montenegro* Arbour argues states are 'no longer holders of a discretionary right to intervene, [but] all States are now burdened with the responsibility to take action under the doctrine of responsibility to protect' and that 'because of the power they wield and due to their global reach, the members of the Security Council, particularly the Permanent Five Members (P5) hold an even heavier responsibility than other States to ensure the protection of civilians everywhere'.[26] Arbour's argumentation is based, however, on a case dealing with genocide. A duty to prevent or stop violations of the other crimes is, as explained, more difficult to establish. The members of the Security Council in the meantime have been reluctant to agree to any kind of measure which may curb their discretionary powers to decide to act or refrain from doing so.[27] Assuming any legally binding obligations on the basis of R2P for all crimes in the second and third pillar therefore seems premature.

Nevertheless as a political commitment it is not without meaning. Burke White notes that 'even without legal obligation, [R2P] is already having concrete impact ... and increased the political and moral costs of inaction in the face of atrocity.'[28] These moral costs stem from the need of the Security Council to maintain its legitimacy. The Security Council's legitimacy is already challenged on several fronts, not least among those is its increasingly unrepresentative composition and the occasional unilateral use of force by powerful states and coalitions, but legitimacy remains central to the power the UN Security Council as it is mainly reliant on this "social capital" to ensure the compliance of states.[29] The political costs involved in neglecting its responsibility under R2P are therefore likely to influence its decisions.

---

[24] The political will to intervene is nevertheless often lacking for a variety of reasons. See for an in depth examination of the United States and its policy regarding different situations in which genocide was perpetrated: Power 2013.

[25] Annan 2000, p. 48; Peters 2009; Peters 2011; Arbour 2008, p. 454; Glanville 2012, p. 20-24.

[26] Arbour 2008, 449-453.

[27] Blätter & Williams 2011, p. 318.

[28] Burke-White 2012, p. 17.

[29] Hurd 2002; Blätter & Williams 2011, p. 312.

This conclusion seems to be supported by the increased frequency with which the Security Council and General Assembly make references to the norm.[30]

The non-binding legal status has not prevented the international community from taking slow but certain steps towards the implementation of R2P. Secretary General Ban Ki-moon has been a norm entrepreneur for the Responsibility to Protect. Through the slogan 'promise less and deliver more' he has urged the UN to start to live up to its rhetoric.[31] However, Vaclav Havel and Desmond Tutu acknowledge 'its implementation remains far from a reality' and they believe the question how the Responsibility to Protect should be implemented to be the most important one remaining.[32] Not only is the implementation process problematized by fears among several states that the concept at some point could be abused by strong powers to meddle unjustifiably in the affairs of smaller states. Other states fear that the concept may restrict states' foreign policy discretion to choose whether and how to act[33] and a lack of political will to stop international crimes forms an enduring problem.[34] Compounding these problems, however, is the fact that there is insufficient empirical knowledge to determine what measures will work when there is the political will to take action. Remedying this problem requires an investigation of the causes of these crimes in order to be able to counteract them.

2. Genocide studies: Instigating international crimes

Several risk factors have been identified which significantly increase the chances international crimes ensue. These include a non-democratic system of government, social schisms in society, a history of violence and difficult life conditions, often entailing political or economic crises and war which will be briefly addressed in turn.[35]

---

[30] Glanville 2012, p. 1-2. For an overview of the relevant resolutions see: International Coalition for the Responsibility to Protect, 'UN Resolutions and Statements on the Responsibility to Protect', <http://www.responsibilitytoprotect.org/index.php/about-rtop/the-un-and-rtop/un-resolutions-and-statements>.

[31] Bellamy 2010, p. 146.

[32] Havel & Tutu 2012, p. xv.

[33] Luck 2009, p. 11.

[34] Williams & Bellamy 2005; Power 2013. Bellamy and Williams more recently, however, spoke of the advent of a new politics of protection which includes a commitment by the international community 'to work through the Security Council to fashion responses to human protection crises': Williams & Bellamy 2011, p. 847.

[35] Rummel 1994; Davenport 1999; Bellamy & McLoughlin 2009, p. 29-34; Fein 1995; Harff 2003, p. 62 and 66; Regan & Henderson 2002; Krain 2000; Kreutz 2006; Alvarez 2001. p. 68-

Rummel in particular has found that the age old adagium 'power kills, absolute power kills absolutely' holds true and concluded that the more dictatorial the regime, the more likely it is to perpetrate mass murder.[36] Others have rather found that there is 'more murder in the middle' and that there is actually a bigger risk for atrocities in states that are in the early stages of becoming more democratic.[37] Overall, however, the consensus seems to be that fully democratic states are the least likely to commit international crimes and more often than not, it seems to be the authoritarian regimes, weak or strong, whom are the worst culprits of this type of violence.[38]

Leo Kuper was perhaps the most prominent scholar to point to a plural society as a necessary precondition.[39] Other scholars have built on this argument and suggested that pre-existing schisms in society can escalate through an increasing dichotomization between 'us' and 'them' which may finally result in the dehumanisation of the other.[40] Sometimes there may also have been previous wars or atrocities which taint the history between those groups and they may provide an added risk factor.[41] Midlarsky argues, for instance, that identifying with the previous perpetrators or the view that the victims in previous rounds of violence were deserving of their fate, can diminish inhibitions to kill again.[42]

A more immediate precursor to violence are difficult life conditions, political or economic crises and war. These difficult life conditions may cause the elite to search out a scapegoat on whom the problems of its citizens can be blamed.[43] War may of course worsen already existing crises but also adds to the risk of mass violence because it provides more opportunities for such violence, brutalises those involved and may serve as a pretext to engage in international crimes.[44] Since democracies are also less likely to wage war, this is another significant reason why democracies will be less likely to perpetrate mass atrocities.[45]

These factors, however, do not make these crimes inevitable. McLoughlin for instance has shown that in several countries which were at risk for mass atrocities, the leader could be instrumental in mitigating these risk factors and prevent violence

---

71; Shaw 2007; Nafziger & Auvinem 2002; Staub 2000, p. 369; Woolf & Hulsizer 2005; Kuper 1981.

[36] Rummel 1994.

[37] Fein 1995.

[38] Krain 2000; Kreutz 2006; Harff 2003; Bellamy & McLoughlin 2009.

[39] Kuper 1981.

[40] Moshman 2007; Sémelin 2003.

[41] Harff 2003; Midlarsky 2005, p. 43-44.

[42] Midlarsky 2005, p. 44.

[43] Alvarez 2001, p. 69; Staub 2000, p. 370.

[44] Nafziger & Auvinem 2002, p. 153; Alvarez 2001, p. 69-71; Shaw 2007; Fein 2000.

[45] Krain 2000, p.46; Kreutz 2006.

from breaking out.[46] In a similar vein, as will be argued below, the leader can also use the risk factors to create a situation in which international crimes actually are perpetrated.

While many of the listed preconditions are relatively common, large scale violence and genocide remain quite rare. Chirot and McCauley explain this predicament by proposing that actual violence requires 'a moral construction'. They argue that human beings are:

'Moralising animals who need to justify their acts. Poverty, disaster, political turmoil, or other painful experiences may anger us, but we will not kill unless we have a specific target, and we must justify our anger toward that target by making its behaviour morally repugnant.'[47]

The moral construction is often provided by an ideology. Ideology in this sense should be understood as shared beliefs and belief systems which not only allow people to make sense of the world but also provides them with a sense of identity and purpose.[48] A given ideology finds its origin in the culture of the society but the belief system can be manipulated. Alvarez explains that:

'To marginalise, disenfranchise, and persecute a group of people requires many citizens to accept the necessity and morality of policies of destruction and this is largely done through the manipulation of belief systems by politicians and others in order to dissimulate, persuade, and mobilize populations in a cause'[49]

The ideology is usually communicated to the population through state propaganda that allows dictators to enhance in-group- out-group schisms and devalue the out groups.[50] This process may lead to dehumanization of the out-group and ultimately to its destruction when they are placed outside of the moral universe.[51] When combined with difficult life conditions which may result in a loss of group pride, frustration and an increase in prejudice, the out-group is easily blamed for society's woes.[52] This played a role for instance in bringing the Nazi party to power in Germany. After Germany had lost WWI they were subject to a peace treaty that they found humiliating and which reduced the standard of living.[53] This period resulted in low self-perception and a rise in anti-Semitism. Jews were blamed, not only for the

---

[46] McLoughlin 2014.
[47] Chirot & McCauley 2010, p. 67.
[48] Alvarez 2008, p. 216.
[49] Alvarez 2008, p. 217.
[50] Smeulers & Grünfeld 2011, p. 248-249.
[51] Woolf & Hulsizer 2005, p. 105; Moshman 2007, p. 131; Fein 1993, p. 82. In the context of torture see: Kelman 1993; Smeulers & Grünfeld 2011.
[52] Woolf & Hulsizer 2005, p. 105; Staub 2000, p. 370.
[53] Staub & Bar-Tal 2003, p. 715.

defeat of Germany in WWI, but for the economic hardship which followed. The Nazi party lost some popularity when a decade later economic and political stability was again established but this was regained after the depression of 1929 set in.[54]

Ideology does not really resonate with the population unless it is made to fit within the already existing culture and myths.[55] Chirot and McCauley explain that 'memory and historical reconstruction, often invented but nevertheless sincerely believed, are important contributors to demands for vengeance of past wrongs that in turn can lead to a new series of mass killings.'[56] To claim, therefore, as some have done,[57] that the mass violence which follows is the result of ancient hatreds is much too simplistic. The dictator can use the influence he holds over the society to give these historical memories contemporary relevance and it is this 'ability to manipulate how the population thinks … and relates to each other' that makes the dictator so powerful.[58] Woolf and Hulsizer argue that this causes the leader to play 'a significant role in moving a culture down a path of mass violence' and Sémelin stresses that in this manner, first and foremost through propaganda, the conditions are created by those in power for the perpetration of the violence.[59]

The dictator does not always need to develop the ideology from scratch. In Serbia for instance, the nationalist ideology was already articulated in a memorandum of the Serbian Academy of Arts and Sciences in 1986. The memorandum warned that Serbs living in Kosovo might fall victim to an impending genocide and advocated creating a greater Serbian state.[60] The document is seen as the 'founding document of modern Serb nationalism' and it is believed that the document was very important in shaping Milosevic' public declarations and policy. Milosevic capitalised on the growing unrest in the country, gaining support from Serbs throughout Yugoslavia for rehashing the ideas from the memorandum.[61]

Staub points out the importance of remembering that the leader is, like the rest of the population, socialised in a particular society and therefore knows its history and cultural sensitivities. This is exactly what 'enables leaders to speak to people's concerns and psychological needs' according to Staub.[62] At the same time, while ideology plays an important role in legitimating the violence, not all dictatorial

[54] Tinsdale a.o. 2002, p. 148.
[55] Tinsdale a.o. 2002, p. 149-50; Sémelin 2003, p. 196.
[56] Chirot & McCauley 2010, p. 91.
[57] Kaplan 2005.
[58] Woolf & Hulsizer 2005, p. 108; Sémelin 2003, p. 196.
[59] Sémelin 2003, p. 206; Woolf & Hulsizer 2005, p. 106.
[60] Morus 2007, p. 143.
[61] Morus 2007, p. 143-60.
[62] Staub 2010, p. 174-75.

leaders that instigate international crimes are ideologically motivated.[63] While some genuinely seem to believe in the ideology they put forward others are more concerned with power, money and prestige. Daniel Chirot developed a typological map where he placed dictators on a scale ranging from extreme ideological certitude to more pragmatic and corrupt tyrants. He mentions Mao Zedong from China, Pol Pot from Cambodia and Adolf Hitler from Nazi Germany as the more ideological leaders and refers to Idi Amin of Uganda as an example of a more pragmatic and corrupt leader.[64]

Certain influential groups may also put pressure on dictators to accommodate their needs and the dictator may resort to mass violence as an easy solution. Robert Mugabe in Zimbabwe for instance was put under pressure from the Zimbabwe Liberation War Veterans Association. They started vying for better living conditions and Mugabe, having relied for support on his own liberation war credentials, caved and started to support their violent farm invasions.[65] While they were not always fully orchestrated by the government, and the government denied involvement, the farm invasions were widely facilitated by them and invaded farms were often given to Mugabe's cronies.[66] For this reason several scholars currently view the veterans, many often being too young to be actual veterans, as a government militia.[67] As this example shows, there is often a fine line between violence that is perpetrated by governmental groups and non-governmental groups on their own initiative and violence that is still perpetrated on behalf of the state.[68] Making use of paramilitary units may provide the state the opportunity to deny any involvement in the crimes and provide them 'plausible deniability'.[69]

Even though international crimes are forms of collective violence, in which many people are involved in some way, often the actual killing is done by smaller units. These may be paramilitary organizations but can also be elite governmental forces as was the case in Greece during the reign of the military junta.[70] Even in the

---

63 Woolf & Hulsizer 2005, p. 107-08.
64 Chirot 1994, p. 167-68.
65 Chan 2003, p. 149-150.
66 Chan 2003, p. 147; Addison & Laakso 2003, p. 464; Compagnon 2011, p. 178-79; Moorcraft 2011, p. 142.
67 Moorcraft 2011, p. 140; Compagnon 2011, p. 65-68.
68 Smeulers 2012, p. 19-22.
69 Ron 2000, p. 287.
The present chapter is, as stated earlier, only concerned with situations in which the state is also the perpetrator of the crimes because it creates the unique situation where the state is no longer capable of acting as a law enforcement mechanism but of course there are also many situations in which the state is not in control and unable to stop international crimes which may be perpetrated by rebel groups. See for instance the distinction made by Smeulers: Smeulers 2012.
70 Gibson & Haritos-Fatouros 1986.

Rwandan genocide, which was characterised by the widespread participation of many people in the killing process, a group that was trained and armed before the start of the genocide, the *Interahamwe*, took the lead in the killings.[71] There are of course also many situations where international crimes are perpetrated without governmental support.[72] This is the case for example when rebels are fighting government forces and in these types of situations the government is not necessarily unwilling but especially unable to live up to its responsibilities under R2P.

However, we can conclude from the foregoing that an authoritarian regime is often not unable but unwilling to stop the commission of international crimes. The dictator then can play an important part in its perpetration. Especially when countries are already at risk due to a history of violence, recent conflict or difficult life conditions, the population is susceptible to an exclusionary ideology that rationalises and legitimates the violence. When the dictator uses propaganda to spread these ideas among the population, and delegates the brutal task of killing and torturing to specialised units, the dictator can create the extraordinary circumstances in which ordinary people come to commit these heinous acts. The state in those situations no longer acts as an inhibiting but as an instigating factor for the perpetration of crimes.

3. Foreign policy analysis: Dictators centre stage

Considering their importance in transforming the risk factors into actual situations of international crimes and the extensive power which they have over their countries working and functioning, dictators should take centre stage in efforts of the international community to stop or mitigate the occurrence of international crimes. Unless overwhelming force is used and the regime is overthrown, success in these situations may often hinge on the reaction of the dictator.

Yet the dominant field of study that analyses how states interact, international relations (IR), has for a long time focused solely on the state, as the dominant and rational actor, rather than the individual.[73] This approach discounted differences between states, making them 'functionally equivalent.'[74] Foreign policy analysis (FPA) challenged this perspective and subsequently drew attention to the actual decision makers.[75] It unveiled the inability of individual decision makers to make such rational considerations and the idea was put forward that rationality was

---

[71] Smeulers & Hoex 2010, p. 441-42.
[72] Smeulers 2012, p. 18-22.
[73] Hudson 2005.
[74] Byman & Pollack 2001, p. 113; Singer 1961, p. 81.
[75] Hudson 2005, p. 2.

bounded.[76] Simon conceptualises bounded rationality as 'behaviour that is adaptive within the constraints imposed *both* by the external situation and by the capacities of the decision maker'.[77]

In the last decade more and more emphasis has been placed on the importance of the individual leader.[78] Especially in authoritarian regimes the leader has an enormous impact on the decisions that are taken within the country because even though they are always reliant on a small circle of essential elite, they have more discretionary power than a democratically elected leader since they are not constrained by their constituents or democratic institutions.[79] There currently is much scholarly work that focuses on dictatorship in general,[80] as well as in depth analyses of individual leaders.[81] However, while there is some discussion to what extent dictators can be characterised as rational[82] the differences in rationality between leaders remained generally unanalysed. This omission is troubling when analysing how international crimes may be countered through foreign policy mechanisms, since ideology sits uncomfortably in the rationality framework.[83] In order to remedy this oversight, it is important to look beyond the boundaries of this discipline.

4. Sociology: Taking the differences into consideration

Because value systems and ideology are neglected even in the more bounded versions of rational choice theories, and because these play such a significant role in the commission of international crimes, a more nuanced conceptualisation of rationality is in order. The work of the authoritative sociologist Max Weber may be very useful in this regard. He has identified two different kinds of rationality. The first of the two types of rational social action, instrumental rationality, most closely resembles what is commonly understood to constitute rational action. According to Weber instrumental rationality is oriented to a 'system of discrete individual ends'[84] The decision maker in this case takes the expectations of the actions of others and

[76] Mintz & DeRouen 2010; Renshon & Renshon 2008; Rosati 2000; Stein 2012; Simon 1985, p. 294.
[77] Simon 1985, p. 294.
[78] Byman & Pollack 2001; Hermann a.o. 2001.
[79] Ezrow & Frantz 2011, p. 149-151; Kinne 2005.
[80] Ezrow & Frantz 2011; Bueno De Mesquita & Smith 2011; Moghaddam 2013; Ayittey 2011; Kets de Vries 2004.
[81] Post 2004; Bullock 1993.
[82] Seliktar & Dutter 2009; Etzioni 2010; Razi 1988; Malici 2011.
[83] D'Avray 2010, p. 41.
[84] Weber 1964, p. 115.

possibly changing circumstances into consideration. He weighs the pros and cons of alternative means and reflects on possible side effects of particular courses of action and on the relative importance of different aims in the decision making process.[85] It allows the decision maker to shift priorities and abandon certain goals when the costs are too high.[86]

Weber allows for the existence of misinformation, strategic errors and the like by introducing the notion that one should assess instrumental rationality subjectively.[87] Because instrumental rationality allows for human error, it does not discard the contributions made by FPA scholars. The advantage of his work, however, is that he allows another type or rationality, which is generally neglected in FPA and IR literature,[88] to exist next to instrumental rationality. When a person acts on the basis of this second type of rationality, value rationality, they act out of

'*…a conscious belief in the absolute value of some ethical, aesthetic, religious, or other form of behaviour, entirely for its own sake and independently of any prospects of external success.*'[89]

The goal is then sacred, it does not allow for compromise and is pursued regardless of the consequences.[90] The person who acts from a value rational orientation feels obligated to act to fulfil certain 'demands' which he feels are required by 'duty, honour, the pursuit of beauty, a religious call, personal loyalty, or the importance of some ''cause'' no matter in what it consists.'[91] Value rationality therefore shows a high degree of commitment to the ultimate value.

Weber pointed out that value rationality and instrumental rationality are not mutually exclusive. He explained that it is possible for instance for a person to try to achieve a value rational goal through instrumental rational means. According to Weber:

'*Choice between alternative and conflicting ends and results may well be determined by considerations of absolute value. In that case, action is rationally oriented to a system of discrete individual ends only in respect of the choice of means.*'[92]

---

[85] Blokland 2006, p. 30.
[86] Varshney 2003.
[87] Norkus 2000, p. 164.
[88] The exception is Stephen J. Morris in: Morris 1999. He mentions the concept sporadically, applying it as a cultural outlook.
[89] Weber 1964, p. 115.
[90] Weber 1964, p. 117; Varshney 2003, p. 86.
[91] Weber 1964, p. 116.
[92] Weber 1964, p. 117.

In this situation it may be expected that the leader may be flexible in the choice of means but is rather determined to fulfil the ultimate objective.

Incorporating Max Weber's findings not only avoids having to assume all decision makers are equally and similarly rational but also allows scholars to incorporate ideological considerations into the decision making process. These different types of rationality are ideal types, analytical tools which cannot be found in reality,[93] but as such are enlightening when analysing the dictator's responsiveness. Since value rational leaders will be much more committed to their goals and will not be concerned with the possible consequences of their actions, they are likely to be less responsive. Borrowing from Max Weber is therefore not only useful to nuance the debate on rationality in the existing literature, but it may also make efforts to bring international crimes to a halt more effective. When deciding on how to stop or mitigate the occurrence of international crimes through foreign policy, it is important to consider what kind of rationality dominates the behaviour of the dictator.

5. Conclusion

Although it is becoming more common, prosecuting leaders that orchestrated mass violence remains a mechanism that is used sparingly. Before trials at international(ised) tribunals are contemplated usually an array of foreign policy mechanisms has been used to try and stop or mitigate the crimes. International criminology should therefore ensure not only to focus on international criminal justice as a mechanism to address these crimes but have a broader outlook that includes efforts to counter these crimes politically as well.

The international community has pledged to prevent and react to halt mass atrocities when a state manifestly fails to protect their populations but its implementation remains far from a reality. Efforts to advance the implementation of R2P and make it more effective should accord a prominent role to the dictator since he often incites these crimes. A history of violence and a cultural enemy can, especially when combined with difficult life conditions, make a population susceptible to exclusionary ideologies but they do not make the crimes inevitable. The dictator, however, often aggravates these risk factors. He can use an exclusionary ideology to create a willingness among the wider population to accept international crimes by rationalising and legitimising the violence. In addition, he may create a willingness to perpetrate the crimes among a smaller subsection of the population, by training

[93] Bailey 1994, p. 17-18.

and arming elite forces or paramilitary groups designated to do most of the actual killing.

It is possible to conclude therefore that ideology is very important in the commission of the crimes, with some of the dictators believing in the ideology they put forward while others do not. Such an ideological outlook, however, sits uncomfortably with contemporary theories on rationality which are said to determine foreign policy decision making. It is for this reason instructive to turn to Max Weber's work to incorporate an alternative conception of rationality that acknowledges people may be much more committed when they strive to attain a goal they find sacred. Taking these differences into consideration shows not all dictators will be equally responsive to foreign policy measures that are targeted to stop or mitigate international crimes and this knowledge may be used to make foreign policy more effective in the future.

Bibliography

Addison & Laakso 2003

T. Addison & L. Laakso, 'The Political Economy of Zimbabwe's Descent into Conflict', *Journal of International Development*, Vol. 15, no. 4 (2003), p. 457-470.

Alvarez 2001

A. Alvarez, *Governments, Citizens and Genocide: A Comparative Interdisciplinary Approach*, Bloomington: Indiana University Press, 2001.

Alvarez 2008

A. Alvarez, 'Destructive Beliefs: Genocide and the Role of Ideology', in: R. Haveman & A. Smeulers (eds.), *Supranational Criminology: Towards a Criminology of International Crimes*, Series Supranational Criminal Law: Capita Selecta, Antwerp: Intersentia, 2008, p. 32-213.

Annan 2000

K. Annan, *'We the Peoples' the Role of the United Nations in the 21st Century*, New York: United Nations, 2000.

Arbour 2008

L. Arbour, 'The Responsibility to Protect as a Duty of Care in International Law and Practice,' *Review of International Studies*, Vol. 34, no. 03 (2008), p. 445-458.

Ayittey 2011

G.B.N. Ayittey, *Defeating Dictators: Fighting Tyranny in Africa and around the World*, New York: Palgrave Macmillan 2011.

Bailey 1994

K.D. Bailey, 'Typologies and Taxonomies: An Introduction to Classification Techniques', in: M.S. Lewis-Beck (ed.), *Quantitative Applications in the Social Sciences*, Thousand Oaks: Sage Publications 1994.

Ban 2009

K. Ban, *Implementing the Responsibility to Protect*, United Nations 2009.

Bellamy 2010

A.J. Bellamy, 'The Responsibility to Protect– Five Years On', *Ethics & International Affairs,* Vol. 24, no. 2 (2010): p. 143-169.

Bellamy & McLoughlin 2009

A.J. Bellamy & S. McLoughlin, *Preventing Genocide and Mass Atrocities: Causes and Paths of Escalation*, St Lucia: Asia-Pacific Centre for the Responsibility to Protect, 2009.

Bellamy & Reike 2010

A.J. Bellamy & R. Reike, 'The Responsibility to Protect and International Law', *Global Responsibility to Protect*, Vol. 2, no. 3 (2010), p. 179-200.

Bischoff, Boas & Reid 2008

J.L. Bischoff, G. Boas & N.L. Reid, *Elements of Crimes under International Law*, 3 vols., Vol. 2, International Criminal Law Practitioner Library Series, Cambridge: Cambridge University Press 2008.

Blätter & Williams 2011

A. Blätter & P.D. Williams, 'The Responsibility Not to Veto', *Global Responsibility to Protect*, Vol. 3, no. 3 (2011), p. 346-351.

Blokland 2006

H.T. Blokland, *Modernization and Its Political Consequences: Weber, Mannheim and Shumpeter*, New Haven: Yale University Press 2006.

Brunnee & Toope 2012

J. Brunnée & S.J. Toope, 'The Responsibility to Protect and the Use of Force: Building Legality?', *Global Responsibility to Protect*, Vol. 2, no. 3 (2010), p. 191-212.

Bueno De Mesquita & Smith 2011

B. Bueno De Mesquita & A. Smith, *The Dictator's Handbook: Why Bad Behaviour Is Almost Always Good Politics*, New York: Public Affairs 2011.

Bullock 1993

A. Bullock, *Hitler and Stalin: Parallel Lives*, New York: Vintage Books (Random House) 1993.

Burke-White 2012

W.W. Burke-White, 'Adoption of the Responsibility to Protect', in: J. Genser and I. Cotler (eds.), *The Responsibility to Protect: The Promise of Stopping Mass Atrocities in Our Time,* Oxford: Oxford University Press 2012.

Byman & Pollack 2001

D.L. Byman & K.M. Pollack, 'Let Us Now Praise Great Men: Bringing the Statesman Back In', *International Security*, Vol. 25, no. 4 (2001), 107-146.

Chan 2003

S. Chan, *Robert Mugabe: A Life of Power and Violence* , London: I.B. Tauris & Co Ltd. 2003.

Chhabra & Zucker 2012

T. Chhabra & J.B. Zucker, 'Defining the Crimes', in: J. Genser and I. Cotler (eds.), *The Responsibility to Protect: The Promise of Stopping Mass Atrocities in Our Time,* Oxford: Oxford University Press, 2012.

Chirot 1994

D. Chirot, *Modern Tyrants: The Power and Prevalence of Evil in Our Age*, New York: The Free Press 1994.

Chirot & McCauley 2010

D. Chirot & C. McCauley, *Why Not Kill Them All? The Logic and Prevention of Mass Political Murder*, Princeton: Princeton University Press, 2010.

Compagnon 2011

D. Compagnon, *A Predictable Tragedy: Robert Mugabe and the Collapse of Zimbabwe*, Philadelphia: University of Pennsylvania Press 2011.

Davenport 1999

C. Davenport, 'Human Rights and the Democratic Proposition', *Journal of Conflict Resolution*, Vol. 43, no. 1 (1999), p. 92-116.

D'Avray 2010

D.L. D'Avray, *Rationalities in History: A Weberian Essay in Comparison*, Cambridge: Cambridge University Press 2010.

Etzioni 2010

A. Etzioni, 'Rational Actors: Neither Mad nor M.A.D.: The Meanings of Rationality, Rogue States and Terrorists', *Defense & Security Analysis*, Vol. 26, no. 4 (2010), p. 431-438.

Ezrow & Frantz 2011

N. Ezrow & E. Frantz, *Dictators and Dictatorships: Understanding Authoritarian Regimes and Their Leaders*, New York: Continuum, 2011.

Fein 1993

H. Fein, 'Accounting for Genocide after 1945: Theories and Some Findings', *International Journal on Minority and Group Rights*, Vol. 1, no. 2 (1993), p. 79-106.

Fein 1995

H. Fein, 'More Murder in the Middle: Life-Integrity Violations and Democracy in the World, 1987', *Human Rights Quarterly*, Vol. 17, no. 1 (1995), p. 170-191.

Fein 2000

H. Fein, 'Civil Wars and Genocide: Paths and Circles', *Human Rights Review*, Vol. 1, no. 3 (2000), p. 49-61.

Gibson & Haritos-Fatouros 1986

J.T. Gibson & M. Haritos-Fatouros, 'The Education of a Torturer: There Is a Cruel Method in the Madness of Teaching People to Torture. Almost Anyone Can Learn It', *Psychology Today*, November (1986).

Glanville 2012

L. Glanville, 'The Responsibility to Protect Beyond Borders,' *Human Rights Law Review*, Vol. 12, no. 1 (2012), p. 1-32.

Harff 2003

B. Harff, 'No Lessons Learned from the Holocaust? Assessing Risks of Genocide and Political Mass Murder since 1955,' *The American Political Science Review*, Vol. 97, no. 1 (2003), p. 57-73.

Haveman & Smeulers 2008

R. Haveman & A. Smeulers, 'Criminology in a State of Denial - Towards a Criminology of International Crimes: Supranational Criminology,' in: Roelof Haveman & Alette Smeulers (eds.), *Supranational Criminology: Towards a Criminology of International Crimes*, Series Supranational Criminal Law: Capita Selecta, Antwerp: Intersentia, 2008, p. 3-26.

Havel & Tutu 2012

V. Havel & D. Tutu, 'Introduction', in J. Genser and I. Cotler (ed.), *The Responsibility to Protect: The Promise of Stopping Mass Atrocities in Our Time,* Oxford: Oxford University Press, 2012.

Hermann et al. 2001

M.G. Hermann et al., 'Who Leads Matters: The Effects of Powerful Individuals', *International Studies Review*, Vol. 3, no. 2 (2001), p. 83-131.

Hudson 2005

V.M. Hudson, 'Foreign Policy Analysis: Actor-Specific Theory and the Ground of International Relations', *Foreign Policy Analysis*, Vol. 1, no. 1 (2005), p. 1-30.

Hurd 2002

I. Hurd, 'Legitimacy, Power, and the Symbolic Life of the UN Security Council', *Global Governance*, Vol. 8, no. 1 (2002), p. 35-51.

Kaplan 2005

R.D. Kaplan, *Balkan Ghosts: A Journey Through History*, New York: Picador 2005.

Kelman 1993

H.C. Kelman, 'The Social Context of Torture: Policy Process and Authority Structure', in: R.D. Crelinston and A.P. Schmid (eds.), *The Politics of Pain: Torturers and Their Masters*, Leiden: COMT 1993.

Kets de Vries 2004

M.F.R. Kets de Vries, *Lessons on Leadership by Terror: Finding Shaka Zulu in the Attic*, Cheltenham: Edward Elgar Publishing Ltd. 2004.

Kinne 2005

B.J. Kinne, 'Decision Making in Autocratic Regimes: A Poliheuristic Perspective', *International Studies Perspectives*, Vol. 6, no. 1 (2005), p. 114-128.

Krain 2000

M. Krain, 'Democracy, Internal War, and State-Sponsored Mass Murder', *Human Rights Review*, Vol. 1, no. 3 (2000), 40-48.

Kreutz 2006

J. Kreutz, 'The Nexus of Democracy, Conflict and the Targeting of Civilians, 1989-2005,' in: Lotta Harbom (ed.), *States in Armed Conflict 2005*, Uppsala: Department of Peace and conflict research 2006.

Kuper 1981

L. Kuper, *Genocide: Its Political Use in the Twentieth Century*, Harmondsworth: Penguin Books 1981.

Luck 2009

E.C. Luck, 'Sovereignty, Choice, and the Responsibility to Protect', *Global Responsibility to Protect* , Vol. 1, no. 1 (2009), p. 10-21.

Luck 2012

E.C. Luck, 'From Promise to Practice: Implementing the Responsibility to Protect,' in: Jared Genser and Irwin Cotler (eds.), *The Responsibility to Protect: The Promise of Stopping Mass Atrocities in Our Time*, Oxford: Oxford University Press, 2012.

Malici 2011

A. Malici, 'The United States and Rogue Leaders', in: Stephen G. Walker, Akan Malici, and Mark Schafer (eds.), *Rethinking Foreign Policy Analysis: States, Leaders, and the Microfoundations of Behavioural International Relations*, New York: Routledge 2011.

McLoughlin 2014

S. McLoughlin, *The Structural Prevention of Mass Atrocities: Understanding Risk and Resilience*, London: Routledge 2014.

Midlarsky 2005

M.I. Midlarsky, *The Killing Trap: Genocide in the Twentieth Century*, Cambridge: Cambridge University Press 2005.

Mintz & DeRouen 2010

A. Mintz & K. DeRouen, *Understanding Foreign Policy Decision Making*, Cambridge: Cambridge University Press 2010.

Moghaddam 2013

F.I. Moghaddam, *The Psychology of Dictatorship*, Washington, DC: American Psychological Association 2013.

Moorcraft 2011

P. Moorcraft, *Mugabe's War Machine: Saving or Savaging Zimbabwe*, Barnsley: Pen & Sword Books Ltd. 2011.

Morris 1999

S.J. Morris, *Why Vietnam Invaded Cambodia: Political Culture and the Causes of War*, Stanford: Stanford University Press 1999.

Morus 2007

C. Morus, 'The Sanu Memorandum: Intellectual Authority and the Constitution of an Exclusive Serbian ''People'' ', *Communication and Critical/Cultural Studies*, Vol. 4, No. 2, June 2007, p. 142-165.

Moshman 2007

D. Moshman, 'Us and Them: Identity and Genocide', *Journal of Theory and Research*, Vol. 7, no. 2 (2007), p. 115-135.

Nafziger & Auvinem 2002

E.W. Nafziger & J. Auvinen, 'Economic Development, Inequality, War, and State Violence', *World Development* 30, no. 2 (2002), p. 153-163.

Norkus 2000

Z. Norkus, 'Max Weber's Interpretive Sociology and Rational Choice Approach', *Rationality and Society*, Vol. 12, no. 3 (2000), p. 259-282.

Peters 2009

A. Peters, 'Humanity as the a and Ω of Sovereignty', *European Journal of International Law*, Vol. 20, no. 3 (2009).

Peters 2011

A. Peters, 'The Security Council's Responsibility to Protect', *International Organizations Law Review*, Vol. 8, no. 1 (2011).

Pictet 1952

J.S. Pictet, *Commentary Published under the General Editorship of Jean S. Pictet*, IV vols., Vol. I, International Committee of the Red Cross 1952.

Pinker 2011

S. Pinker, *The Better Angels of Our Nature: Why Violence Has Declined,* London: Viking, 2011.

Post 2004

J.M. Post, *Leaders and Their Followers in a Dangerous World: The Psychology of Political Behaviour*, Ithaca: Cornell University Press 2004.

Power 2013

S. Power, *A Problem from Hell: America and the Age of Genocide* , New York: Basic Books 2013.

Razi 1988

G.H. Razi, 'An Alternative Paradigm to State Rationality in Foreign Policy: The Iran-Iraq War', *The Western Political Quarterly*, Vol. 41, no. 4 (1988), p. 689-723.

Regan & Henderson 2002

P.M. Regan & E.A. Henderson, 'Democracy, Threats and Political Repression in Developing Countries: Are Democracies Internally Less Violent?,' *Third World Quarterly*, Vol. 23, no. 1 (2002), p. 119-136.

Renshon & Renshon 2008

J. Renshon & S.A. Renshon, 'The Theory and Practice of Foreign Policy Decision Making', *Political Psychology*, Vol. 29, no. 4, 2008.

Ron 2000

J. Ron, 'Territoriality and Plausible Deniability: Serbian Paramilitaries in the Bosnian War', in: B.B. Campbell and A.D. Brenner (eds.), *Death Squads in Global Perspective: Murder with Deniability*, New York: Palgrave MacMillan 2000.

Rosati 2000

J.A. Rosati, 'The Power of Human Cognition in the Study of World Politics', *International Studies Review*, Vol. 2, no. 3 (2000), p. 45-75.

Rummel 1994

R.J. Rummel, 'Power, Genocide and Mass Murder', *Journal of Peace Research,* Vol. 31, no. 1 (1994) p. 1-10.

Sadat 2011

L. Nadya Sadat (ed.), *Forging a Convention for Crimes against Humanity*, Cambridge: Cambridge University Press, 2011.

Seliktar & Dutter 2009

O. Seliktar & L.E. Dutter, 'Assessing the Rationality of Autocrats: The Case of Saddam Hussein', *International Journal of Intelligence and Counter Intelligence*, Vol. 22, no. 2 (2009), p. 275-297.

Sémelin 2003

J. Sémelin, 'Toward a Vocabulary of Massacre and Genocide', *Journal of Genocide Research*, Vol. 5, no. 2 (2003), p. 193-210.

Shaw 2007

M. Shaw, 'The General Hybridity of War and Genocide', *Journal of Genocide Research*, Vol. 9, no. 3 (2007), p. 461-473.

Simon 1985

H.A Simon, 'Human Nature in Politics: The Dialogue of Psychology with Political Science.' *The American Political Science Review*, Vol. 79, no. 2 (1985), p. 293-304.

Singer 1961

D.J. Singer, 'The Level-of-Analysis Problem in International Relations', *World Politics* 14, no. Special Issue 01 (1961), p. 77-92.

Smeulers 2012

A. Smeulers, *In opdracht van de staat: gezagsgetrouwe criminelen en internationale misdrijven*, Tilburg: Tilburg University 2012.

Smeulers & Grünfeld 2011

A. Smeulers & F. Grünfeld, *International Crimes and Other Gross Human Rights Violations: A Multi- and Interdisciplinary Textbook*, Leiden: Martinus Nijhoff Publishers, 2011.

Smeulers & Hoex 2010

A. Smeulers & L. Hoex, 'Studying the Microdynamics of the Rwandan Genocide', *British Journal of Criminology*, Vol. 50, no. 3 (2010), p. 435-454.

Stahn 2007

C. Stahn, 'Responsibility to Protect: Political Rhetoric or Emerging Legal Norm?' *The American Journal of International Law,* Vol. 101, no. 1 (2007), p. 99-120.

Staub 2000

E. Staub, ‘Genocide and Mass Killing: Origins, Prevention, Healing and Reconciliation’, *Political Psychology,* Vol. 21, no. 2 (2000), p. 367-382.

Staub 2010

E. Staub, *Overcoming Evil,* Oxford: Oxford University Press 2010.

Staub & Bar-Tal 2003

E. Staub & D. Bar-Tal, ‘Genocide, Mass Killing and Intractable Conflict’, in: D.O. Sears, L. Huddy & R. Jervis (eds.), *Oxford Handbook of Political Psychology,* Oxford: Oxford University Press 2003.

Stein 2012

J. Stein, ‘Foreign Policy Decision Making: Rational, Psychological and Neurological Models’, in: S. Smith, A. Hadfield & T. Dunne (eds.), *Foreign Policy: Theories, Actors,* Oxford: Oxford University Press 2012, 130-46.

Tinsdale et al. 2002

R. Scott Tindale et al., ‘Group Processes and the Holocaust’, in: L.S. Newman and R. Erber (eds.), *Understanding Genocide: The Social Psychology of the Holocaust,* Oxford: Oxford University Press 2002.

Varshney 2003

A. Varshney, ‘Nationalism, Ethnic Conflict, and Rationality’, *Perspectives on Politics,* Vol.1, no. 1 (2003), p. 85-99.

Weber 1964

M. Weber, *The Theory of Social and Economic Organization,* Translated by Talcott Parsons A.M. Henderson, New York: The Free Press 1964.

Williams & Bellamy 2005

P.D. Williams & A.J. Bellamy, ‘The Responsibility to Protect and the Crisis in Darfur’, *Security Dialogue* 36, no. 1 (March 1, 2005), p. 27-47.

Williams & Bellamy 2011

P.D. Williams & A.J. Bellamy, 'The New Politics of Protection? Côte D'ivoire, Libya and the Responsibility to Protect', *International Affairs*, Vol. 87, no. 4 (2011), p. 825-850.

Woolf & Hulsizer 2005

L.M. Woolf & M.R. Hulsizer, 'Psychosocial Roots of Genocide: Risk, Prevention, and Intervention,' *Journal of Genocide Research*, Vol. 7, no. 1 (2005), p. 101-128.